NONE
BE LOST
Oliver V. Dalaba

GOSPEL PUBLISHING HOUSE
SPRINGFIELD, MISSOURI
02-0621

ACKNOWLEDGMENT

A word of appreciation is given to Sylvia Lee for writing chapter 7, "Enrollment Plus."

Library of Congress Catalog Card Number 77-074553
International Standard Book Number 0-88243-621-X
Printed in the United States of America

Preface

No man has a monopoly on truth. It is only as we receive more of Jesus, who is the way, the truth, and the life, that we have anything to share with others. This book is written with the sincere desire to share Jesus Christ in the best way possible with the most people possible. No pretense is made in assuming that it contains all the answers. In fact, after it was written the writer already saw areas where additions should be made.

It is probably true that there is nothing constant but change. Sometimes, change seems to repeat itself, but that very change may be new to someone else—a new convert, a new generation—a new package for the eternal truth. I like the way Fulton W. Buntain puts it:

> The building of a great church demands a philosophy, a reason for being. What is the primary reason for the existence of the church in the world today? "To reach the most number of people, in the best possible way, with the claims and teachings of Jesus Christ."
>
> All the programs of the church should constantly be focused on that philosophy. In reaching large numbers of people we must constantly use the best possible ways—ways that do not bring reproach upon the work of God; ways that genuinely work. It must constantly be remembered that the message of the church is the answer to the basic needs of the human life.
>
> Our problem is not our message but its packaging and delivery. Jesus promised that if He would be lifted up He would draw

all men unto Him. Therefore, we must develop programs that will introduce people to Christ. This can be accomplished through the reading of the Bible, the atmosphere of the church service, the discussion group, the small home group, the great evangelistic effort, and through our lives as individual Christians.

It has been said that man looks for better methods and God looks for better men—men and women of vision who are not afraid to try new packaging methods and are willing to change the "delivery system" to reach the intended goal.

Certainly it is basic that to build a great church that church must be a nonjudgmental group of believers who accept people where they are and at the stage of growth they are. Certainly Jesus gave us this example. Dare we do less?

As you read through this book, let it stimulate your own thinking. The God who created man made him in His own likeness. Let that creative thinking in you lead you into new areas of effectively sharing the gospel. Remember: Others may teach the gospel better than you, but no one can teach a better gospel than you!

Contents

1 So Send I You

The highest aspiration of any Christian is to be like his Lord and Saviour, Jesus Christ. We were made in the image and likeness of God. Jesus said: "Follow me and I will make you fishers of men" (Matthew 4:19).

After the successful completion of redemption at Calvary and His subsequent resurrection, Jesus took the opportunity to restate His disciples' mission in life. They were to be "sent ones": "As my Father hath sent me, even so send I you" (John 20:21). In this passage their purpose is stated, the authority is delegated, and the victory is assured. The voice of the Creator has spoken.

As we consider the mandate for evangelism (our very reason for writing this book), let's give consideration to the following areas: (1) the commission; (2) the concept; (3) the compassion; and (4) the continuity of evangelism.

The Commission

If we are to fulfill the task of evangelism to which we are commissioned, it is important for us to understand the full scope of the word. The dictionary defines *commission* as: "1. The act of committing, doing, or perpetrating; positive doing; contrasted with omission. 2. The act of entrusting; the matter entrusted; a trust, charge. 3. A certificate which confers a particular authority; conferring rank as in armed forces. 4. A body of persons acting under public authority. 5. The transaction of business for another under his authority, agency. 6. The compensation of an agent."

I think the whole gamut of the above definition and more is included in the Great Commission of Christ to His disciples—both the early disciples and today's disciples. Matthew 28:18-20 reads like this:

> And Jesus came and spake unto them, saying, All power is given unto me in heaven and in earth. Go ye therefore, and teach all nations, baptizing them in the name of the Father, and of the Son, and of the Holy Ghost: teaching them to observe all things whatsoever I have commanded you: and, lo, I am with you alway, even unto the end of the world. Amen.

Mark 16:15, 16 puts it quickly into focus with the "sent ones'" responsibility and the hearers' responsibility: "And he said unto them, Go ye into all the world, and preach the gospel to every creature. He that believeth and is baptized shall be saved; but he that believeth not shall be damned."

The authority in our commission is God. He is omniscient (all-knowing); therefore, I can accept His direction with full confidence. He is omnipotent (all-powerful); I need never fear failure for lack of provision or divine support. He is omnipresent (everywhere at once). There is no place on earth where I will be outside the scope of His authority or assistance.

The rank of our commission is our relationship to God. We are sons of God. This speaks of our eternal family ties. We are joint-heirs with Jesus. Our inheritance is incorruptible. We are emissaries to the world. We represent Christ wherever we go.

The scope of our commission is specific and all-inclusive. Our function is the propagation of the gospel, the good news of salvation. It is to be shared with all men, in all places, until Christ returns.

Compensation is promised to us in the fulfillment of our task. Eternal life is ours. John 3:16 says: "For God so loved the world, that he gave his only begotten Son, that whosoever believeth in him should not perish, but have everlasting life."

How wonderful to be commissioned by God to represent Him on earth. How awesome is our task to tell all men. How accountable we are for the souls we come in contact with and the gifts and enablings God endows us with. To be commissioned in the ranks of the redeemed and to be led by a never-failing Captain gives credence to the potential victory we seek. We are not alone in our task and must unitedly press forward with our mutual responsibility.

Hebrews 12:1 states: "Wherefore, seeing we also are compassed about with so great a cloud of witnesses, let us lay aside every weight and the sin which doth so easily beset us, and let us run with patience the race that is set before us."

The Concept

"And I, if I be lifted up from the earth, will draw all men unto me" (John 12:32). In essence, this is evangelism—presenting Christ, lifting Him up, exposing people to Him. We must let men see His person, His provision, His power, and His plan, and bring them into an atmosphere or place of decision where Christ's drawing power (and not our efforts at rehabilitation) can effect a life-changing experience. This indicates the priority we must give to Jesus and the self-effacing quality of a good soul winner.

Recycling

We are all conscious of the fact that when a product has either fulfilled or failed its function, it is considered waste. Too often it is simply discarded. Recvcling plants can take this waste material and so completely change it that it becomes a completely new product. Jesus said as much to Nicodemus in John 3: "Ye must be born again [recycled]" (v. 7).

Our call to evangelism sends us in search of wasted lives and social rejects. To that one who has failed miserably, we present new life in Christ. To the older person who feels his life is behind him, we open new vistas on God's horizon.

Personal Relationship With God a Prerequisite

Jesus said to Peter in Luke 22:32: "When thou art converted, strengthen thy brethren." In Matthew 15:14 we read: "If the blind lead the blind, both shall fall into the ditch."

While God's Word has inherent powers of persuasion, it is most effectively used by one whose life is also a testimony of God's redemption. When I as a soul winner am where I should be in God, I can then be used of God to help others.

Love Is Motivation for Soul Winning

Jesus said to Peter in John 21:15, 16: "Lovest thou me . . . ? . . . Feed my lambs. . . . Lovest thou me? . . . Feed my sheep."

We are speaking here primarily of our love for Jesus being our basic motive for soul winning. Jesus said our love for Him will effect our follow-up of new converts ("feed my lambs"). It will promote maturity in the saints ("feed my sheep"). A healthy flock will bear new lambs. Evangelism is well-balanced in its outreach and follow-up.

Evangelism Is Based on Invitation

Luke 14:16-24 gives us a rather vivid portrayal of evangelism:

1. Provision: "A certain man made a great supper."
2. Invitation: ". . . And bade many."
3. Reminders: " . . . Sent his servant. . . . "
4. Rejection: "They all with one consent began to make excuse."
5. New Outreach: "Go out quickly into the streets and lanes of the city."
6. Evaluation: "Yet there is room."
7. Extended-outreach evangelism: "Go out into the highways and hedges, and compel them to come in."
8. Ultimate results: a. Those who rejected the invitation shall not eat of the supper.

   b. My house may be filled.

The parable is quite explicit in revealing that Jesus came first to the Jews who rejected Him. He then turned to the Gentiles with a first and second appeal, which could well speak of the Early Church and the current Church; the early and the latter rain.

What speaks to me so loudly, however, is the outline of evangelism for the Church. We have many who are aware of God's provision. They have grown up either in the church or in the shadow of the church. They have received the invitation to come to Christ and partake of His benefits, but prefer to involve themselves in business and social ventures.

God's faithfulness sends them reminders of the lateness of the hour and the need for immediate response through personal witness. If those who grow up in the church don't respond to God's current revival, He will turn anew to those who may never have heard the invitation before.

This outreach, He says, should be systematic: "Into the streets and lanes of the city." People from the main streets and side alleys alike are invited to God's table for "communion" with Him. There should be times when the workers evaluate whether or not they have covered their entire city (their "Jerusalem"). Then they should begin to extend their invitation to the countryside round about (all "Judea"). This includes personal contact on the street, mail evangelism, radio and T.V. ministries, and extension classes, with an ever-broadening circle of coverage.

With compelling attitude and action we are to remind men and women that to partake of God's provision demands response to God's invitation. The inevitable judgment, or time of separation, is just as sure as the Marriage Supper of the Lamb.

Meal-sharing Evangelism

Jesus had a knack of meeting people where they were. He recognized the futility of trying to impart spiritual concepts to a man with an empty stomach. He also knew the value of a home atmosphere and physical preparedness in evangelism. Jesus used mealtime for evangelism and evangelism follow-up so much that some called Him a glutton.

1. *Jesus' example.* First, Jesus used meal sharing as a time to show friendliness to Matthew, a tax collector (Matthew 9:9-13). It was only a matter of time until many of Matthew's associates joined them at the house. These city servants were more accustomed to criticism than to kindness, but Jesus used this occasion to share kindness and the gospel.

Second, we see Jesus going to Zaccheus' house (Luke 19:5-10). Here Jesus plainly stated His purpose of using a meal as a time of soul winning. "This day is salvation come to this house, forasmuch as he also is a son of Abraham. For the Son of man is come to seek and to save that which was lost" (vv. 9, 10).

The result was obvious. The life of Zaccheus was

revolutionized. The lost was found. The crooked tax collector confessed his faults and made restitution. A life of selfishness was exchanged for one of generosity. All of this took place, not in church, but in a meal-sharing situation.

Third, Jesus used meal sharing as an opportunity for counseling (John 21:12-25). This counseling session was designed to produce soul winners. As Jesus shared bread and fish upon the fire, He soon got to His main objective. When they had dined, Jesus said, "You also need to feed my sheep and lambs."

2. *Jesus' teaching.* Not only did Jesus practice meal-sharing evangelism, He also taught it. He outlines some important guidelines in Luke 14:12-14. Don't just share with your friends, relatives, or rich neighbors, but minister to the needs of the poor, the maimed, the lame, and the blind. Evangelism must reach all people of all classes and it must involve us in something as personal as sharing around our own table.

3. *Early Church.* The Early Church started out to follow this practice of meal-sharing evangelism. They went daily from house to house breaking bread. They ate their meat with gladness and singleness of heart. They had all things common and shared with those in need, physically and spiritually.

A dark shadow appeared on the horizon of evangelism as the church became selective or picky about who they would eat with. Peter was called to task for eating with the uncircumcised (Acts 11:1-3). He defended this type of evangelism by stating that the Holy Ghost descended on them as He had on the disciples in the Upper Room (vv. 4-18).

In Galatians 2:11, 12, however, this pioneer of meal-sharing evangelism, this early evangelist to the outsider, begins to backtrack on his position. When some men criticized him for eating with the Gentiles, he withdrew and separated himself, fearing them which were of the circumcision.

The Bible indicates that we have to be continually on guard lest we fall into a rut in such a simple thing as meal sharing, and forget that He has given us a blessed opportunity to share Christ and to share fellowship. We need to share Christ with our new neighbors. We need to share the hope of the gospel with those in need. We need to share fellowship with our new members.

Someday we all hope to share in the great meal-sharing time, the Marriage Supper of the Lamb. Until that time, let's share together in remembrance of Him around the Communion table in church and the dinner table in the home.

4. *Dinner exchange.* Here's one way we have used to help accomplish a part of this plan. In February or March of each year, we ask all those interested in participating in a dinner exchange to put their name, address, and phone number, together with the number of persons in their family, on a slip of paper. These are all placed in a box and mixed together. Each family then draws a slip from the box and invites that family to dinner sometime during the month. In this way, every family then becomes a host and a guest. Many new acquaintances are formed and friendships established. Sometimes a Sunday school class decides to do this just among themselves and their newcomers.

Let's not forget, however, that this is only part of the solution. We also recognize that many persons have fragmented families and may be lonely on Thanksgiving Day. Our old-fashioned Thanksgiving with turkey roasted on the open fire and families who wish to share bringing foodstuffs together, is open to all. The atmosphere of people in early American costumes and a spirit of love helps to share the brotherhood made possible through Jesus Christ.

Add to this a men's prayer breakfast, a mother-daughter banquet, a father-son banquet, a few afterglows, a senior-citizens' dinner, a few wedding receptions, and several funeral dinners, and we realize that we can share Christ very effectively.

But what about your home? Maybe you could invite the parents of one of your pupils home for dinner and share Christ. Maybe by taking a meal to a family in need or to a new neighbor, you can say by positive action, "Jesus Christ cares and we care about you."

The Compassion of Evangelism

Compassion is defined as:* "That drawing and agitation of the innermost parts at the sight of any distress or miserable object. It causes revolting action in the innermost being to bring deliverance from such unlawful and inhuman misery and suffering."

We read of the compassion of Christ nine times in the Gospels: Matthew 9:36; 14:14; 15:32; 20:34; Mark 1:41; 5:19; 6:34; 8:2; and Luke 7:13.

I think it is interesting to note that the compassion of Jesus motivated Him to action. In Matthew 4:13-22, on His first trip to Galilee, He shared the light of the gospel and preached repentance. His compassion compelled Him to enlist disciples to assist Him. Capernaum was the base of operations.

On His second tour of Galilee He broadened His outreach (v. 23) and went about all Galilee. His approach is outlined for us: (1) teaching, (2) preaching, and (3) healing. We catch a glimpse of His compassion for soul and body. He never forgot His priorities.

In Matthew 9:35-38 on His third tour of Galilee, Jesus used a very similar approach to evangelism:

Teaching—To instruct; to impart knowledge; to instill doctrine; to explain. Jesus had something to say.

He illustrated His material and He permitted and answered questions.

Preaching—To herald as a public crier, to proclaim. Preaching calls attention to truth; teaching is the work of making it clear.

Healing—This was Jesus' ministry. His concern for human need was genuine and His power sufficient. His grace made it available.

Matthew gives us insight into His nature. This was no political ploy on the part of Jesus. He was moved with compassion. It is here we see stated what John expounds on further in John 10—Jesus had a shepherd's heart. He was always touched by the fainting, the scattered, and the leaderless ones.

Here also we see evangelism pictured as a great harvest (Matthew 9:37, 38). The harvest is great, the time is vital, the laborers are needed but few, and God is the Director of the harvest and the Employer of the workers. We must imbibe the compassionate heart of Jesus if we are to effectively work in today's harvest field.

Compassion for the Individual

In John 11 we read the touching story of Lazarus. Jesus wept. The compassion of Jesus was deeply stirred for one He knew and loved. In time of bereavement, He ministered to a family. His own emotional involvement was seen by them and their friends. During this experience, Jesus never lost sight of His high calling—evangelism. He must share God in the hour of crisis with His loved ones and their friends, even to the point of overcoming His own grief through ministry. Jesus used the graveside scene to evangelize (vv. 41, 42, 45).

Compassion for the City and the Multitude

The emotions of Jesus were stirred deeply by Israel's rejection. As He stood looking at the capital city, the awesome results of that mass rejection gripped His entire being (Matthew 23:37). His compassionate heart cried out for their salvation and lamented their loss.

True compassion takes no satisfaction in raw justice, but still cares even though love receives no satisfactory response. The knowledge that there were other sheep in another fold did not lessen Christ's compassion for Jerusalem. Our mandate for evangelism is compassion, not a search for accepting surroundings.

Our Compassion

To catch a glimpse of the compassionate heart of Jesus gives us a feeling of acceptance and security. That's only a portion of the picture, however. We must reflect that compassion and acceptance to those we meet. When I accept myself (my birth, my potential, my limitations) I see the importance of being part of the family of God. I must also realize that others need to be accepted.

Suicide is running rampant among youth and is now rising among preteens. Dope addiction is a menace. Rebellion is a syndrome of rejection. Runaways reflect a search for acceptance. Despair, defeatism, and disappointment surround us. Ours is a ministry of reconciliation.

Classroom Compassion

Our classes need to show compassion. Children coming from broken homes need reassurance and love. A few words of personal interest and a loving hug can make them feel wanted and open them to your lesson.

Kids from good homes need affirmation in their position which seems so different from the world.

Compassion Guidelines

As children grow into youth, our compassion needs to be shown in teaching them how to find acceptance. The withdrawn person must be shown love without strings attached. The overperformer should not be rejected but involved. The following guidelines for peer-group acceptance could be shared:

1. Be accepted by being a true friend.
2. Be accepted by carrying your share of responsibility.
3. Be accepted by making valid contributions to group projects.
4. Be like Jonathan who accepted David even though David received the kingdom he perhaps desired and was in line to inherit.
5. Be like Luke who accepted Paul although their skills were vastly different (2 Timothy 4:11). Learn how to fill supporting roles.
6. Reassure them of divine acceptance. God accepted His work at Creation (Genesis 1:31). He accepts the prayers of His people. He accepted Elijah's sacrifice on Mt. Carmel and the sacrifice of Jesus on Calvary. He accepted the requests for healing by blind Bartimeus and a woman with an issue of blood.

He accepts us in salvation "just as we are." Not because of good works, a fancy pedigree, or rehabilitation, but He accepts us just as we are. That takes compassion on the part of God and it takes compassion on the part of a teacher. That type of compassion needs to radiate from our lessons and our attitude in the classroom.

Continuity of Evangelism

The Early Church had a great beginning. With a burst of evangelism that could be compared to a meteor in the sky flashing light to the darkened world, the early apostles and witnesses shared their faith. It was a world of slavery, heartbreak, disease, poverty, and Roman domination. Following the teachings of Jesus that they were to shine as lights in the darkness, these men and women of God brought answers to their troubled world. They taught freedom in Christ, hope for tomorrow, healing for body and soul, riches in heaven, and about the kingdom of God that is within as well as the one to come.

Evangelism Needed

As we look at our world today, we see the need for continued evangelism. Population growth presents fresh challenges around the globe. Many are starving. People have traded one set of masters for another. The cry for liberty and justice for all still rings. Food is in short supply in many places. As Jesus said: "The poor always ye have with you" (John 12:8).

Families are divided. Communication has broken down and many institutions are falling in the wake. Youth is copping out on life with drug addiction, alcohol, indiscriminate sex, and even suicide. Child abuse is a major problem. Education is failing to meet the need of the person to adjust to life.

Governmental corruption has shaken our land with feelings of insecurity. World government is talked about as a solution, but it does not deal with the heart of man. Politics, economics, environment, and national security expand their slogans and budgets, but fail to bring peace of mind.

Churchmen of the world disagree over social issues.

We face reevaluation of the church's role in our society and possible loss of favored tax status. New religious cults are popping up and ancient cults and paganism are sending missionaries to our shores to fill a spiritual vacuum.

Yes, we still need evangelism. The world of Jesus' day was in need. The Early Church faced a formidable task. Ours is no less important. Jesus declared to His world of hopelessness: "Be of good cheer; I have overcome the world" (John 16:33). To the helpless disciples He offered His Spirit. He has not recalled this gift to the Church. The world needs evangelism. We need the compassion and spirit of Christ to carry on the evangelistic effort in our century and in our towns.

Evangelism Practiced by Jesus

Four times Jesus toured Galilee. He showed us the importance of continuity in evangelism. He returned again and again to the same places and faced similar needs. He had faith in His solution and was not afraid to offer it again and again.

In his personal outreach ministry we observe Jesus talking to Zaccheus, giving him a public and personal invitation. He didn't let it stop there. He followed this up with a visit to the man's house. Here is an example of making the most of every opportunity.

Nicodemus was met during the night hours. Jesus could have said, "I teach during the day. That fulfills my responsibility. If Nicodemus really wants to hear me, let him come to the regular services." But Jesus had a different attitude. His evangelistic thrust was continuous—anyone, at any place, anytime.

We could also refer to His teaching in the temple over and over again, in spite of rejection. He took the children on His lap. He touched them. His concern was felt. But He not only touched the beautiful children,

He also touched the diseased leper. Evangelism was a continuous practice.

Pursued by the Apostles

When Jesus went away He left a plan behind for the continuity of evangelism. It included men. The apostles were filled with the Spirit. Daily they prayed, taught, and witnessed. It wasn't long until intense persecution made them count the cost of evangelism. Pay it, they would—some in prison, some with stripes, and some with their very lives. But persecution did not stop evangelism. Like beating a fire, it only spread the sparks and soon the witness of Christ sprang up wherever the scattered witnesses chanced to land.

Some sowed the seed. Their missionary journeys are classic in dedication and effectiveness. Others followed to teach the Word. We liken them to those who water the seed. Others followed to help in the harvest, but it was God who gave the increase. Evangelism is not our program, it is God's, and He will continue it until He returns.

Some declared: "We are of Paul, we are of Cephas, we are of Apollos" (1 Corinthians 1:12). How important for us not to turn evangelism into a personality contest. It must be carried out with divine fervor, be divinely directed, and return the glory to God.

Current Hopes of the Church

"When the Son of man cometh, shall he find faith on the earth?" (Luke 18:8). Yes; a thousand times, yes. He has not imparted to us a stagnant faith. Our message is not one of historical rhetoric but eternal hope. Our goals are not to achieve artificial status symbols, but to speak in the power and demonstration of the Spirit. The Church Christ returns for will be alive and well.

Summary

What a challenge is ours! We have been commissioned by God to evangelize the world. Jesus gave us the instruction in person. He demonstrated the compassion that must motivate us. He practiced the concepts that still work today. Our task is not done when our family is saved or our church crowded. Our work must continue until Jesus comes.

---

*Finis Jennings Dake, *Dake's Annotated Reference Bible* (Lawrenceville, GA: Dake Bible Sales, Inc.), p. 9.

2 Smorgasbord of Methods

How can we make contact with those who need the gospel most? What do you do about fitting the Sunday school message to those who come from such varied backgrounds? I'm tired! How can I get help and helpers? These kids know the story better than I do. Can't we put them to work in some way?

Here are a few of the various philosophies of outreach:

1. We'll light a fire of evangelism under those we have until they become powerful soul winners.
2. We are going to use the media: newspaper—letters to the editor, paid ads; radio—bought time, sponsored programs, children's story hour; T.V.; billboards.
3. Direct-mail approach—bulletins, correspondence courses, form letters, personal letters.
4. The fourth group may use the phone—tell-a-thons, dial-a-soul, "Here's Life, America," teachers' weekly check-up by phone.
5. Bring them in—busing, car pools, no-excuse day.
6. Extravaganzas
7. Bring them in to get saved, or get them saved and bring them in.
8. Extended revival campaigns for the whole family.
9. Specialized evangelism.

Seventy Sent (Luke 10:1-17)

As great as Jesus was, He enlisted the services of others to help propagate the gospel.

Their services were preparatory to the personal ministry of Jesus himself. Luke tells us the Seventy were sent two by two into every city where Jesus himself would come. Their ministry was more than advance publicity (though it contained that aspect), because they were instructed to heal the sick as well as declare that "the kingdom of God is come nigh unto you" (v. 9).

Throughout history God has used a variety of people, and they have used a variety of methods in evangelism.

Abraham used a twofold approach in saving Lot. His method depended on the situation. On one occasion he armed his servants and personally led a rescue party to help in a time of physical danger and dilemma (Genesis 14). When the matter could only be spiritually resolved, Abraham prayed to God until he received an answer (18:16-33).

Moses was an organizer. He followed the practical advice of his father-in-law, Jethro, and set up a justice system that would involve many accountable persons with himself as a court of last resort (Exodus 18). He received a system of laws directly from God and instructed the people in their application. He also knew the value of prayer and used this method until he reached a point of exhaustion. Aaron and Hur, sensing his burden and his limitations, held up his hands until the victory was won (17:12).

Gideon, directed by God, had great goals, but accomplished them with limited personnel who were highly committed (Judges 7). They were not adverse to trying new methods.

David used a recognition of God's timing as well as God's anointing to bring him to a place of success.

Jesus discipled a few "who were with Him" to carry on His work. For special outreach programs he used a boy and his lunch, a converted prostitute, a tax collector, and an advance guard of 70—many methods for many men.

Extended ministry, or ministry that reaches out, must carry with it a concern for man's need, a dependence on divine assistance, organizational structure, proper timing, committed personnel, and a flexible approach.

Billy Sunday was quite methodical in preparing for evangelism. His advance men enlisted the churches of the city and set up a series of committees: ladies' groups, men's groups, businessmen, advertising, prayer, finance, Sunday school teachers, and follow-up. He built a specially designed tabernacle for the revival campaign, complete with sounding board, acoustics, and fire escape doors at the end of every aisle. His manner was to the point and colorful enough to hold interest. Billy recognized the need for people to be discipled into the church. This is where follow-up committees become involved.

As Sunday school workers, we should take advantage of every city-wide campaign in our town in which the gospel is preached and every revival sponsored by our church. It is not a case of church vs. Sunday school in a race to see who can do it best while the other drags its feet, but a cooperative approach by every facet of the church body. Sunday school teachers and pupils as altar workers and as follow-up committees—what a ready-made structure for evangelism!

In his day, Wesley traveled far and wide preaching the gospel, leaving churches and preaching stations along his trail. We have passed the horse-and-buggy days, but we have not outgrown our need for outreach evangelism.

Busing

Twentieth-century evangelists drive their cars down side roads and city streets in search of the unconverted and the unchurched. "Come ride our bus" is the approach of some, while others park their buses at certain locations at specific times and conduct Sunday school on the spot. Still others, facing crowded facilities or needing time to integrate new pupils into the regular school, bus their prospects to the parking lot of the church, where age-groups are divided and classes are conducted in the buses.

What about busing as a tool of evangelism? For many it has been the answer. For others trying to duplicate someone else's success, it has been frustration.

1. If you are considering busing, you should first make a list of the equipment needed, the materials you will use, and the sources of supply. A couple of good books on the subject of busing should be purchased and perused. *All About the Bus Ministry* and *Keep the Bus Ministry Rolling* by Wally Beebe are two books to be considered (Murfreesboro, TN: Sword of the Lord Publishers).

Some proponents of busing state emphatically that a minimum of three buses should be purchased and three routes established. This, they say, will stimulate competition and also help ensure success. If the attendance of one route is down, another may be up. This provides encouragement for the others.

2. Second, you should take an inventory of your church's personality. Is busing something you have the personnel to handle? Are your teachers equipped to cope with a sudden influx of kids with no Bible background? Are your pupils emotionally and spiritually prepared to accept the newcomers or will you stir up more conflict than you can offset with prayer and diplomacy?

What are your options to reach the community if you don't try busing? Will your community ever be reached if you don't bus? Is your official church board familiar with and in favor of the concept? Are you committed to at least a year of active work at this program to determine its effectiveness?

3. Third, personnel should be enlisted and trained before implementing your busing program. Perhaps you can send your workers to visit a Sunday school already using the busing program successfully. Some churches bring in an experienced leader to conduct an in-depth seminar in their own church. A state of expectancy should be created in each class and special ministries prepared for regular pupils. Strive to develop the regulars and create a desire for evangelism in them while reaching out for the lost sheep.

Visitation is the backbone of the busing program. Well-outlined routes, planned conversational approaches at the doors of prospects, and consistent follow-up of prospective pupils are mandatory for success. Some schools are employing the visitation aspects of busing without the buses. Neighborhood car pools or total-family enrollment have proven to be successful in increased evangelism—sort of a busless busing program!

Busing can be an effective tool of evangelism. Make sure your involvement is based on compassion and commitment and not "me-too-ism." Its successes are not automatic, but come as a result of much prayer, dedicated workers, and a climate that is right for this particular outreach tool.

Extension Classes

Can Sunday school go beyond the church doors? Yes! An enterprising extension superintendent can establish effective classes in restaurants, nursing homes, private homes, and modular classrooms. He can also enroll a sizable list of shut-ins who can be taught the Sunday school lesson at home each week. This takes trained and committed personnel.

There is a tendency to substitute a brief worship service or sharing time for the lesson and then call it Sunday school. This is a mistake. Worship is needed and sharing is important, but whether an extension class is in a classroom or the home of a shut-in, the need for a lesson is still there. The Word and instruction in it have eternal value.

Apartment Evangelism

Cities present unique situations. Tight security in high-rise apartments can almost make door-to-door evangelism a thing of the past. A careful study of each city or each apartment complex can result, however, in gratifying results. Setting appointments by phone or mail may give entrance to a few key homes in each apartment complex. They in turn can help to evangelize their ("Jerusalem") home area.

Establishing rapport with a landlord or manager can open opportunities for special children's programs within the apartment complex itself or their community center building. Archie Marshall has done a very effective job in this area. His materials and approach are worthy of your consideration.

Happy House

A "Happy House" is a portable ministry center on wheels. A set of trailer wheels forms the base. A brightly painted little house sits on top. Its sides open up to display puppets, gospel magic, and a screen for films and filmstrips. Flannelgraph stories, cassette stories, and whatever you may desire to feature, are also housed in the "Happy House."

It can be easily pulled from playground to parking lots adjacent to apartments or to parks and fairgrounds. Arrangements should be made with city officials or owners for any permits that might be required in your particular area.

Happy-sounding music and intriguing commercials from an outside speaker can bring the kids running, like the Pied Piper of Hamlin. Once the crowd gathers, the message of Christ can be shared. Remember: The purpose is evangelism, not just entertainment.

Fairs

The Sunday school should not ignore its outreach opportunity at the county or state fair. Contact the appropriate officials or committees early (from 6 months to 1 year in advance) and reserve a booth at the fair.

Involve your pupils in preparing decorative displays. Train them for literature distribution and personal evangelism. Have prayer meetings for several weeks before the fair. Make a list of the things you will need to take. Assign pupils areas and times of responsibility. Remind them and their parents of their involvement in plenty of time for them to make plans.

Parades

I still recall the time I prepared a float for Royal Rangers and drove it in the Memorial Day parade. An auxiliary fire-policeman followed me into the driveway and inquired: "What's Royal Rangers?" After a brief explanation he said that he wanted his boy involved. His entire family is now saved and involved in the church. He moved up through the local outpost to become a sectional commander.

Parades are golden opportunities for Sunday schools to enter preaching-teaching floats. Pupils can be involved in the preparation of the float as well as the parade itself. Colorful banners, good music, and marching feet can complement a well-prepared float and serve notice to your community that you care.

Handicapped

Nearly every community has some who are handicapped. Maybe you will meet them at a special school. Perhaps they live next door to some of your pupils. What plans can you make to reach them? In school, it can be a special program. Your pupils could prepare a skit, some songs, and some special gifts. Perhaps you have one in your midst who is artistic or good with puppets. Gospel magic or lessons from chemistry can all be used effectively.

A social could be arranged to which the handicapped are invited. Special games should be provided with them in mind. Care should be taken that you give the necessary assistance without being overprotective.

In your class, be sure to take time for the handicapped. Their reactions may not be as rapid as your other pupils. Let them know you love them. Avoid situations where they feel like the ugly duckling. If planning a new building, don't forget ramps for the wheelchair pupil. Maybe they can be installed in existing facilities.

Hardness of hearing and slowness of speech are handicaps you should be alert for. Blindness or partial blindness locks a pupil into a strange world. We have to make a special effort to project ourselves into his field of awareness Stories of Christ and His treatment of the handicapped have special significance. Special care must be taken to assure the handicapped of God's love.

Day School

Christian day schools are springing up with amazing

speed. Need for discipline, inability of children to read, biased teaching about creation and evolution, and slipping morals with its attendant problems in the public schools, have been cited as some of the reasons for a massive rush to Christian schools. Here are a few things you should consider if you are contemplating a Christian school:

1. Check your area to determine needs for a school.
2. Contact the state for basic requirements.
3. Consider the relationship of the school to the total church and its departments.
4. Give consideration to financial feasibility.
5. Evaluate current facilities and future needs.
6. Decide on Accelerated Christian Education (A.C.E.) or a conventional system.

But what about evangelism? Probably half of your enrollment in a Christian school will come from families outside your church. Many of them will be completely unchurched. Parent-teachers' fellowship, booster clubs, and auxiliaries provide numerous opportunities for soul winners to rub shoulders with the unconverted. Special programs, whether seasonal in nature or specially planned, can present a message of hope and truth. Students themselves become carry-home evangelists. The truths they learn in class or chapel and the papers they take home can be the means of opening a home for Christ.

Sunday school workers should be careful not to create a feeling of antagonism with day-school pupils, and day-school staff should exercise similar caution in reference to Sunday school. Though there may be some overlapping, we need to recognize that in many instances our facilities serve two different groups.

Room atmosphere is important, attitude is vital, and a

recognition that both are needed is crucial. Day-school teachers can be very good Sunday school teachers. Beware, however, of overexposure to the same pupils on Sunday as during the week. Adverse attitudes could develop in some pupils.

An evangelistic Sunday school will consider the homes of day-school pupils as prospects for evangelism and Sunday school enrollments. Follow-up on a consistent basis will indicate a genuine concern.

Vacation Bible School

In looking at V.B.S. as an outreach tool, it is probably important for us to break it down into categories—purpose, planning, personnel, and program.

Purpose

The person who doesn't know what he wants to accomplish will never know if he reaches his goal.

Does V.B.S. exist to keep kids off the street for a few hours for a week or two during summer vacation? Is it designed to be a baby-sitting service for frustrated parents? Are our goals traditional continuity? Or is there a motivation to reach the unsaved and train the ones we have in evangelistic technique?

I have long been impressed with the poem that suggests that it is just as important to build a fence at the top of the cliff as it is to park an ambulance down in the valley. The story of "Muddy Feet" (available from the national Sunday School Office) has also left its mark on my mind.

The purpose, as I see it, for V.B.S. is twofold. First, it is a training ground for current and potential soul winners. It helps to build a bulwark of defense around vulnerable youth, impressionable children, and spiritual newcomers.

In a concentrated 2-week school a teacher can have

as much impact on a young life as is possible in many months of Sunday school. Biblical concepts are reinforced by practical doing, such as handcrafts, missions emphasis, and the teacher's sharing of the gospel. Game time provides opportunity to practice the principles of social behavior taught by Jesus Christ. The Psalmist said: "Thy word have I hid in mine heart, that I might not sin against thee" (Psalm 119:11).

A second purpose of V.B.S. is evangelism or salvaging those who may have fallen off the cliff of spiritual priority. God's Word penetrates the soul and brings conviction. Attendance contests stimulate boys and girls to bring others. Names are added to prospect files. Entire homes are opened to the gospel. Decision time finds response in many young and tender hearts. V.B.S. purposes to share Christ and minister to the needs of children, and at the same time it involves adults in maturation through Christian service.

Planning

I don't think we can overemphasize the importance of planning ahead for V.B.S. Very early in the year, no later than March, the Sunday school executive committee should begin laying plans for this summer outreach. A date should be selected and integrated into the total church calendar. A director should be chosen, contacted, and his or her acceptance confirmed. Sample V.B.S. materials should be ordered and evaluated. Soon thereafter, departmental directors should be selected and a meeting held to consider areas of need and emphasis.

Two months before V.B.S., teachers and workers should be chosen and primary publicity begun. Workers should review materials and plan supplemental helps with which they are particularly adept. Following this, leaders should anticipate pupil enrollment and order student books and handcraft supplies. Con-

tingency plans should be made for unexpected enrollments. Can we borrow from another church? Will a
phone call to our supplier render quick delivery? Shall
we vary our teaching method for a day until new
supplies arrive?

Publicity should continue and be increased in accordance with the nearness of your calendar date.
Church bulletins, letters to parents, radio, newspapers,
posters, skits in Sunday school and church, T.V., and
personal invitation should all be employed where feasible. Before you open your V.B.S., the entire staff
should meet for orientation and a total review of the
program, schedule, discipline, transportation, and
goals. It is a great time to pray for a real evangelistic
thrust.

Personnel

Adequate personnel is important. Quality is crucial.
As the responsible committee considers a V.B.S. director it must ask the question: Does this person care
about souls? This has to be number one if you are
planning for evangelism. Add to this, organizational
ability, communication skills, up-front confidence, a
cooperative spirit, and a touch of diplomacy, and you
have gone a long way toward ensuring success.

Departmental directors are also key persons. Not
only should they contain similar qualifications as the
director, but they should be well versed in their area of
responsibility. Knowing their subject matter is vital but
being aware of the characteristics and social needs of
their age-group is equally important. They should have
some degree of experience, or at least a willingness to
start well ahead in personal preparation.

They will need to be alert for problem areas in their
department and act decisively in finding solutions.

They should keep in communication with the director without bugging him or her over simple details that they can handle themselves. Departmental directors should endeavor to build evangelistic fervor in their department and a sense of unity within the whole school.

Teachers should be enlisted who have a genuine testimony of Christian experience and a desire to teach the age-group they're assigned to. It does not necessarily have to be the same age or class they teach in Sunday school. Some teachers are available for V.B.S. who may not be able to teach all year long. If you are planning to have helpers in each class, strive to find those who are compatible with each other. This will avoid unnecessary conflicts and encourage your teacher in the pursuit of her task.

Don't forget handcraft instructors who know their craft. All thumbs and two left feet will contribute to a messy room and wasted supplies. They should also think of their work in terms of evangelism. Getting close to a boy on a project may build the confidence needed to reach a lad the lesson has not penetrated.

Recreational personnel should be more than people who like to play. They should be mature enough, spiritually and emotionally, to lend reinforcement to lesson concepts. These people need to be included in your prayer time for evangelism as much as your teachers. Recreation is not just a time filler; it is an opportunity for evangelism.

Program

Much of the schedule you follow and the activities you include in your V.B.S. will be dictated by the curriculum you select. It is vital that you choose curriculum with evangelistic aspects and doctrinal truth. I am happy to endorse Word of Life literature from Gospel Publishing House.

No matter what curriculum you choose, however, it cannot do the job by itself. It needs to be evaluated, understood, internalized, and adapted to local needs.

A V.B.S. program should start with stimulating opening sessions. They should contain dignity, inspiration, discipline, and variety. A number of persons and presentations should be employed. Singing should be capably directed and total participation encouraged.

During a 2-week V.B.S. there could be several guest appearances by persons with special talents. A Bible reading to the whole school emphasizes the priority we place on this Book. Don't drag the opening or the classes beyond their allotted time. Be punctual, well disciplined, and dependable. Schedules are designed to serve us. This requires cooperation by every department and activity group.

One of the important program areas is the commencement. Many parents and friends will be in attendance. Plan your commencement with simplicity and punch. Don't try to require so much of your kids that they get frustrated, and don't let your program drag until discipline is forfeited. Plan at least one feature that encompasses evangelistic truth. This should be presented by someone who is capable and prepared. Provide time for commitment but don't drag out the appeal until resentment builds to the point that you sacrifice future opportunities to reach these parents.

Kids Krusades

Kids Krusades will never replace V.B.S. They are both geared primarily to children but each is unique in itself. While V.B.S. is evangelism through teaching, doing, and recreation, Kids Krusades are evangelism in a one-place setting. They follow a progressive theme that climaxes with an altar call at the conclusion of each service. This, of course, may vary with each individual children's evangelist, but Kids Krusades are beneficial in a church-setting evangelism effort.

Advantages of Kids Krusades

1. *Timing*—One of the advantages of Kids Krusades is the flexibility of timing involved. They can be successfully conducted almost any time of year. Often we tie a Kids Krusade in with a revival meeting for adults. This can be done successfully, however, only if you have facilities capable of housing both activities at the same time and adequate personnel to coordinate the efforts. While V.B.S. is usually tied to vacation periods during the summer, Kids Krusades can be held in the early evening hours even while school is in session.

2. *Limited personnel*—There are many good children's evangelists who specialize in this field. And yet there is still room for many more. A man or woman who is able to communicate with children or a husband-and-wife team with their varied skills can conduct a program for several hundred kids at one time with a minimum of discipline difficulty.

Enough local help should be enlisted to take attendance and secure addresses of prospects. A few more adults should be scattered throughout the congregation of children to help with any emergency situations. Whereas a V.B.S. demands a large staff of teachers and workers, a Kids Krusade can be held with a limited number of workers and doesn't require as much home preparation.

3. *Many prospects*—The excitement of a Kids Krusade with its lively songs, interesting filmstrips, puppets, gospel magic, flannelgraph stories or chalk drawings, and roleplaying skits lends itself easily to attendance contests. This will bring a host of newcomers to almost any church, large or small. Often, parents of newcomers will sit in on a service to observe what

their kids are seeing and become interested in the church program. Canvassing a neighborhood with promotional leaflets announcing the crusade or even a parade of kids with banners will stir excitement. It is not uncommon for a Kids Krusade to double and triple its size from the first night to the last.

4. *Worship setting*—The similarity of a Kids Krusade to church services leads to a natural climax with an altar call. While some children may simply follow the lead of others in going forward, a large number of genuine conversions will take place. It is important for the crusade director not to overemphasize the emotional aspect of the altar call but to lay down clear guidelines of commitment.

Children should be instructed that if they have already accepted Jesus as their personal Saviour they do not need to be saved again every night. Many a Kids Krusade has also resulted in several receiving the baptism in the Holy Spirit during the prayertime following the dismissal of the main body in attendance.

Disadvantages

Here are a few areas you need to consider:

1. *Mere entertainment*—Some persons who specialize in child evangelism make the mistake of substituting intrigue for conviction. If you use magic, don't forget the spiritual application. Should puppets or a ventriloquist's dummy be your vehicle of communication, balance your humor with truth. In the area of songs, don't forget to use some that teach as well as inspire action. Children should leave a Kids Krusade not saying, "Wasn't he great!" but, "Isn't Jesus wonderful!" Jesus said: "If I be lifted up from the earth, [I] will draw all men unto me" (John 12:32).

2. *Church segregation*—Another point to be on guard against is the tendency to let the evangelist, the

director, or a select few persons from your church carry the whole load. There may be other activities that cannot be postponed during a crusade, but as much as possible, the entire church should be made aware of what is taking place and enlisted in prayer and transportation support.

If you are conducting a dual revival (kids and adults) part of the problem is already solved. Kids Krusade week is not a time for a Royal Ranger camp-out or Missionettes tour. Integrate your Kids Krusade in the total church calendar and plan well in advance.

SAMPLE PROGRAM

Introduction of evangelist or director by host pastor. Welcome and introductory remarks by evangelist.

Theme chorus (standing)
Prayer (standing)
Chorus time—2 or 3 choruses (standing or sitting depending on choruses)
Gospel magic—3 ropes, teaching unity
Chorus
Memory work—visualized or magnetic board
Chorus
Puppets or ventriloquist's dummy
   —teaching honesty
   —dummy makes announcements
Offering—boy and girl hold plates for march
Filmstrip—while offering is counted
Chorus
Offering report—"Race to the Moon": red rocket, boys; blue rocket, girls (sounds on tape)
Chorus
Story—flannelgraph, illustrated message, or chalkboard drawing
Altar call

There are many variations possible. My observation and experience has been that you should not linger too long on any one type of presentation. A generous supply of choruses while the children are standing helps to relieve their "fidgets." Storytime or the main presentation may involve roleplaying, a ventriloquist's dummy, or a flannelgraph or chalk drawing, but whichever you choose, it should lead to a serious, spiritual climax.

Resources

Nearly every well-equipped Christian bookstore has some helps available for those who want to work with children. You may be interested, however, in the following addresses:

The Tarbell's Course in Magic, Louis Tannen, Publisher, 120 W. 42nd Street, New York, New York.

Christian Visuals, 6421 Hasbrouck Avenue, Philadelphia, Pennsylvania 19111.

Triquet Paper Company, 201 North Hosmer, Lansing, Michigan 48912 (Bogus paper for chalk artists).

Industrial Research Corporation, Middleton, Wisconsin 53562 (Flash Paper).

Story Hours

A family living room or basement recreation room can provide another valuable outreach opportunity. Those with child evangelism at heart but with limited access to public buildings may start an effective neighborhood story hour right in their own homes.

Resource materials may be secured from Gospel Publishing House, Youth for Christ, Child Evangelism, or your local Christian bookstore. Don't overlook the materials that may be stored in your church library or Sunday school supply room. Many good pictures can be secured from magazines which may be useful in illustrating your own series of Bible stories.

Consistency is a valuable asset in story-hour ministry, as it is in many others. The person who starts with a bang but cancels every other week or two will soon have nothing to cancel.

Variety of presentation should follow some basic theme. After instructing for a while in the requirements of salvation and inspiring by well-illustrated stories, don't forget to take time for decisions. Evangelism is no accident. It is the direct result of man acting as God's agent in reconciliation (2 Corinthians 5:20).

Summary

Jesus began a great work (Acts 1:1). He didn't start this work and teaching only to have it falter and stop. His great work continues. Through the agency of the Holy Spirit believers now carry on the work and teaching Jesus began. As we are all different in our personalities, so will our approaches to evangelism differ. Whether we get them saved and bring them in or bring them in to get them saved, let's make sure we have a plan that we put to work.

Be consistent in evangelism, but use variety in your approach. People have personalities too and each will relate to a different approach. We are His hand extended. In personal witness or group effort we can expect success. We are not here to do it alone. It is His work, we are just His hands.

3   Loaves and Fishes

It had been a long day. Five thousand men besides women and children had traveled on foot from their cities. They were in a desert place. Many were sick and all were hungry. Jesus had ministered to the sick, but there still remained some very practical needs.

It was now about 3:00 p.m.—the time of the evening sacrifice—and Jesus' disciples were at the point of admitting they didn't know how to meet the needs of the people who were there. Quite simply, Jesus commanded: "Give ye them to eat." Their reply was, in essence: "But we can't, Lord. We don't have the necessary provisions and we don't know how to share effectively what little we do have." "Bring what you do have to me," said Jesus, "and I will make it sufficient."

The crowd of people was told to sit (expectantly) in preparation for the evening meal. Jesus blessed, broke, and gave to His disciples the necessary supplies to fulfill what He had previously commanded them to do— "Give ye them to eat." (See Matthew 14:15-21.)

I guess this is where I get a large portion of my philosophy of Christian service: *Do your best and God will do the rest.*

God knows exactly how well-prepared or how ill-prepared we are. He sees the needs of evangelism and service. He asks us to give Him what we have and enter into a partnership with Him to minister to the needs of people.

In considering some practical helps for evangelism, it seems that we often find ourselves in a similar dilemma: Our field is a desert with inadequate sources of supply. The hour is growing late and natural solutions seem impossible. The crowds in need are great and growingly receptive. Humanly speaking we sometimes feel frustrated in the very moment we see our greatest opportunity to minister to existing needs.

Well, let's bring such as we have to Christ. Let Him bless it, break it, multiply it, and give it back to us again in sufficient supply to meet the needs of those He sends us to.

Let's take a look now at some of the loaves and fishes (tools of evangelism) that we have to present to Jesus for His blessing.

Witnessing Plans

Marked New Testament

A noted physician was once asked what he would do if he had only 4 minutes in which to perform an operation on which a man's life depended. He replied, "I would spend the first 2 minutes deciding what to do and how to do it."

Most persons who fail in evangelism do so because they simply fail to plan for it.

Here's how I have my pocket New Testament marked. It follows the plan outlined in the Royal Ranger's Leadership-training Course Number II with one addition:

1. Romans 3:23
2. Romans 6:23
3. John 1:12
4. 1 John 1:9
5. Revelation 3:20
6. 1 John 5:10-13

At the bottom of the page of the first reference, I list

the next reference or page number I wish to use. I shade the verse with a yellow pencil for easy finding and put a cellophane tape tab on the page for easy turning.

This preparation gives you assurance when you witness and it also tells the person to whom you are witnessing that you cared enough to prepare.

Every person must find his own way of explaining verses or expressing their purpose but basically, I say something like this:

1. Romans 3:23: "For all have sinned, and come short of the glory of God."

We have all done many things right, but we all come up a little bit short in some areas. Like a 20-foot ladder being just too short to reach a 24-foot roof; or $2 being just too short to pay for an item costing $2.25, so we come short of meeting God's standards. "I need help! A longer ladder, a little more cash; can someone help me?" That's my condition.

2. Romans 6:23: "For the wages of sin is death; but the gift of God is eternal life through Jesus Christ our Lord."

Every man who works expects to be paid. He doesn't work for one employer and get paid by another. If I labor in sin I will be paid the wages of sin—death—eternal separation from God.

I can't buy salvation, I already know I have come up short. No good works or good intentions can put me on God's payroll. I need someone to help me out—a gift from someone who cares. That's what God did for me. He gave me the gift of His Son, Jesus—the gift of eternal life.

3. John 1:12: "But as many as received him, to them gave he power to become the sons of God, even to them that believe on his name."

If I'm a little short on the ability to pay and someone

offers to pay for me, an outright gift, I have only one thing to do. That's receive it. When I of my own free will accept or receive Christ He gives me power to be part of God's family. I can believe in a Name like that.

4. 1 John 1:9: "If we confess our sins, he is faithful and just to forgive us our sins, and to cleanse us from all unrighteousness."

Here's another way of putting it. God can't help me till I tell Him what my need is. He never invades our privacy. Though He knows all, He won't go against our will. If you tell Him that you know you have come up short, that you have sinned, He will never use it against you to put you down. He forgives you and lifts you up.

5. Revelation 3:20: "Behold, I stand at the door, and knock: if any man hear my voice, and open the door, I will come in to him, and will sup with him, and he with me."

If a friend of yours knocked at your door at mealtime what would you do? Jesus wants to live in your life, share in your conversation, and be a part of your daily life-style as much as your daily meals. He wants in and you're the only one who can make that possible. Would you like to right now? Let's pray together: "Dear Jesus, I know I have sinned, and I need a Saviour. I believe You died on the cross for me. I accept You as my Saviour. Live in my life and by Your help I will live for You. Thank You for this gift of eternal life. Amen."

What has happened to you now? Are you saved? Do you feel saved? Well let me show you something in God's Word that is greater than feelings. It's what He has to say about what has happened to you.

6. 1 John 5:10-13: "He that believeth on the Son of God hath the witness in himself: he that believeth not God hath made him a liar; because he believeth not the record that God gave of his Son. And this is the record, that God hath given to us eternal life, and this life is in his Son. He that hath the Son hath life; and he that hath

not the Son of God hath not life. These things have I written unto you that believe on the name of the Son of God; that ye may know that ye have eternal life, and that ye may believe on the name of the Son of God."

God just wants to reassure you that He keeps His end of the bargain. He wants you to know that you have eternal life based on His Word and your belief on His Son, Jesus Christ.

Roman Road

Here's a similar plan that has been used very effectively by many. Salvation is pictured as a road. Matthew 7:13, 14: "Enter ye in at the strait gate: for wide is the gate, and broad is the way, that leadeth to destruction, and many there be which go in thereat: because strait is the gate, and narrow is the way, which leadeth unto life, and few there be that find it."

A person needs to follow God's road to salvation in much the same way people followed the Roman roads in the days of Jesus.

1. Man's need—Romans 3:23
2. Sin's penalty—Romans 6:23
3. God's provision—Romans 5:8
4. Man's response—Romans 10:9

This is simple, to the point, and all in one Book. The point of decision is standing at the crossroads, deciding which way to go.

The Gospel Hand (Walter Wiemer)

1. God loves you (John 3:16).
2. All have sinned (Romans 3:23).
3. Christ died to pay for your sin (1 Cor. 15:3).
4. Believe Christ died for your sin (John 1:12).
5. When you believe you receive everlasting life (Romans 6:23).

These basic facts can be illustrated by the five fingers

on one hand and are especially helpful in witnessing to children.

Using the outline of John 3:16, the middle finger represents God's love, the index finger stands for the world, and the thumb stands for God's Son. All our other fingers are helpless without the thumb. The ring finger represents the sinner who accepts Jesus Christ and the little finger stands for the assurance of eternal life. In his book *Evangelize Thru Christian Education,* Elmer Towns gives a very thorough explanation of this plan (Wheaton, IL: Evangelical Teacher Training Association, 1970).

Graphic Witnessing Guide

The Men's Department of The General Council of the Assemblies of God has produced a very effective witnessing tool called the Graphic Witnessing Guide. It is available in large flip-chart form for instruction or the small pocket-size for personal witnessing. After using this tool, it can be given to the prospect as a reminder of what you have shared with him.

Steps to Peace With God (Billy Graham)

This is a nice plan to leave with someone for further study.

Four Spiritual Laws (Bill Bright)

This has been used very effectively in the nation-wide campaign "Here's Life America." There is a leader's or soul winner's guide for use on the phone as well as the handy pocket-size booklet for personal handout.

Bill Glass

The Bill Glass Evangelistic Association uses a similar plan. The key point, I think, is the training that is involved in preparation for the actual use.

Wordless Book

This is for kids or those with limited backgrounds. Out of construction paper, fasten the following sheets together for a visual help in witnessing to children:

Black—sin.

Red—blood of Jesus shed on the cross.

White—clean heart: The blood of Jesus cleanseth from all sin.

Gold—heaven: Streets are paved with gold. No sin can enter there.

Green—growth: A tree is alive and growing. Jesus wants us to grow.

These are a few of the many witnessing plans available. The important thing is that you choose one and prepare to use it. Practice your plan and then put it into continual operation. You may supplement your basic plan with some of the others, depending on the age of the prospect or the situation.

Witnessing Places

Part of the miracle of loaves and fishes is the setting in which it was performed—a desert place. Far from ordinary sources of supply, Jesus rallied His disciples to resourcefulness, the ultimate resource being God himself. When we have taken inventory and our evaluation shows us lacking, let's try Jesus. When our supplies are inadequate and our fellowman is wrestling with similar problems, don't give up—give it to Jesus.

Community

Every community is different. Culture affects openness or close-mindedness toward the gospel. Certain approaches will work in one city but will fall flat in another.

Paul recognized this in his approach to evangelism. To the Romans he spoke of government, authority, and structure. To the Greeks he talked of philosophy and declared the unknown God. To the Jews he opened the Old Testament Scriptures. But above all else he remembered his main message: "I determined not to know anything among you, save Jesus Christ, and him crucified" (1 Corinthians 2:2). Let your message of evangelism be anchored to the Rock, but geared to the times. Let the packaging be current, but the product eternal.

To the farmer Jesus spoke of wheat, corn, and weeds. He referred to sowing, watering, and reaping. To temple personnel, Jesus spoke of its construction and place in Jewish life and revealed himself as the Temple of God. To the fisherman, Jesus spoke of catching men. Whatever the setting, Jesus geared His message to the familiar and led His hearers to the related but transcendent truths.

Within the geographic boundaries of any city or rural area there may be a variety of communities. Ethnic background, industry, business, school, or recreational opportunities may segregate neighbors into a series of communities. Age-levels will determine approach. Educational levels will dictate curriculum and language. Work and leisure interests provide different motivational needs for different communities. Our evangelistic outreach must consider our entire community with its variety of subcommunities.

Whether your miracle is needed in a desert place or fishing village; whether it must reach a woman of the streets or a college professor; bring what you have to Jesus and let Him work the miracle.

Some Sunday school classes have organized effectively to share their witness in the community. Hospital parking lots, shopping centers, nursing homes, schools, and parks all provide places where we can meet people. High-rise housing for the aged, low-cost housing projects, and individual homes are more of the places where we need to come face-to-face with the challenge to evangelize.

Parking lots are good places for literature distribution. On special occasions a particular space may be reserved with management and some interesting display arranged to get attention. Class members could be on hand to distribute literature and counsel with those who ask questions.

If no space allocations are made, the car-door-hanger or literature-insertion-under-a-windshield-wiper approach can be used. Being careful not to block doorways or become a nuisance, some persons can be very effective distributing literature at major access areas of a shopping center or bank. These occasions are probably most effective if tied to some special event at your church or some seasonal or calendar event, such as Pentecost Sunday, the Fourth of July, Thanksgiving, or Christmas. Halloween time, when many are asking for treats, is a great time to reverse the order and share a treat; i.e., the Word of God in pamphlet form.

Nursing homes and senior-citizen apartments seem always ready to welcome children. One or two well-prepared songs can be used over and over effectively in key locations, and followed up by visits to rooms or apartments of occupants who are unable to gather in a group setting. Prior planning is a must, of course.

Capitalizing on our bicentennial celebration in 1976, our church planned a big day for the Fourth of July, with a series of extended meetings leading up to and following the big day. Royal Rangers were involved building signal towers on the front lawn and camping on the site as a public witness. A large sign hung between the two signal towers, telling what was happening.

Door knockers in the shape of Liberty Bells gave pictures and information regarding the bicentennial celebration. Sunday school workers went door to door giving these personal invitations to those they met and leaving the Liberty Bell program hanging on the door where no one answered the bell. This was personal involvement of many in a great event, and supplemented newspaper, radio, and T.V. advertising. Not only did we have a great day, but at least one family we know of is now in the church simply because they found the program invitation on their door when they returned home.

We also help to evangelize our community when we get involved with community needs. The Salvation Army, with its food baskets and assistance in temporary housing, is always looking for additional help from our churches. They are glad to use your baskets and your personnel in delivering them. What open doors for evangelism! Giving to "Goodwill" enterprises could be followed up with a class visit to their headquarters. This may lead to new prospects for home visits or on-the-spot evangelism.

Well-planned programs will often find a ready opening in the school system. Though this may vary from place to place, don't overlook the possibility of an "assembly" at your local school.

If you have a message to share, there will always be a place to share it. Even in prison, Paul witnessed to his keepers and won many to Jesus Christ. The work of God is not bound.

The Classroom

The Sunday school classroom may be one of the best places for evangelism. There are usually a few committed Christians in *each* class. They can help set the atmosphere for evangelism. There are usually several unsaved who enter the classroom during any given year. They are the prospects for evangelism.

Does your classroom atmosphere accurately and compellingly present Christ? Do you have posters that preach, people who care, and programs that challenge? Friendly, get-acquainted times make a newcomer feel at home. Pupils who read the Scriptures and pray in the classroom remove the "sissy" image many persons fear in their peer group.

Lessons that are well prepared and flexible enough to include a newcomer's needs, under the Holy Spirit's guidance, can convince a person of his need for Christ. Time set aside for recommitment and new commitments can reap a bountiful harvest. For the shy person the teacher may wish to invite those with questions to linger after class for discussion. Pupils may also reach other pupils if they have prayed and prepared for the opportunity.

A class newspaper can be helpful in binding a class together and thus setting the atmosphere for evangelism. As students do a little homework on an exciting class project, they are stimulated to think and to share. Probably a monthly paper would take sufficient time. Some might prefer to do one on a quarterly basis.

Those who don't feel inclined to start a class newspaper might like to make a scrapbook. Each pupil can contribute throughout the year. Subject areas could be designated for salvation, healing, the Holy Spirit, Christian growth, and the second coming of Christ. A review of material submitted can be a great springboard for evangelism. A pupil may be asked to explain publicly why he brought or wrote a particular article. This provides a witness to those who are listening. Or the teacher may choose to comment on the meaning of the articles, cartoons, pictures, or poems submitted by the class members.

Lesson materials are important vehicles for evangelism. Some lessons may lend themselves more easily than others to classroom evangelism, but every lesson leaves room for something this important. The primary lesson aim may be instruction in Christian living, but the soul-winning teacher will plan ahead for group and personal evangelism.

This assumes that a teacher gets to know his class. It would be fruitless to aim for conversion when he knows that everyone there is saved. It does, however, make it easy for the Holy Spirit to lead you when you have prepared with evangelism in mind. Be spiritually alert for salvation needs in your classroom and don't assume that everyone there is automatically saved just because he or she grew up in the church.

Class Socials

Fellowship is an important aspect of the Christian life. Your pupils need a time of getting together outside the classroom. They also need to see you in a different setting occasionally. God made us social creatures. There are many benefits of togetherness. I should like to suggest that the class social is not only a time for fellowship and fun but also for evangelism.

Many unsaved, "fringe" members, and uncommitted will attend a class social who may seldom be seen in Sunday school or church. The challenge then is to win them at the social. You can't come on too strong in the opening moments of your evening's activities, but a class social should never close without some witness for Christ.

Perhaps this witness will be seen in a prayertime that commits the evening to God and seeks His care and guidance. It may be planned into some of the games—Bible baseball, name that gospel tune, or charades using Biblical characters. It could also be presented in a brief devotional by one of the class members. A teacher's summary remarks may point out the benefits of the Christian life and give opportunity for personal inquiry following the close of the activities. Class members themselves are a witness by the way they conduct themselves as well as what they say. They should be encouraged to stay alert for personal witnessing opportunities.

The Church

Evangelistically minded Sunday school classes will not limit their efforts to their own classroom or social. They will become active participants in all outreach activities of the church. During a revival meeting, for instance, a teacher may designate a particular night for her entire class to sit together in the service. Pupils may strive for 100 percent attendance and also be encouraged to bring their friends. Extrinsic and intrinsic motivation may be employed depending on the situation. An alert class might designate some member from the class to be at each entrance to welcome those they believe to be in their age-group. An invitation to attend their Sunday school class could be given in written or oral form.

Evangelism should not be limited to being present, welcoming newcomers, or bringing friends. It should have a conscious effect on church behavior. It should stimulate a prayerful attitude and create a friendly atmosphere. The desire for evangelism should reach a peak at altar time—no rushing out the door, no whispering in the seats, no distracting actions, but a meaningful time of prayer for unsaved members of the class.

With discretion, a concerned member of the class could invite his or her friend to go forward, offering to go with him. If there are pupils at the altar whose age approximates your class' age-group, positive encouragement by a peer may be all that is needed to solidify the intentions expressed by a response to the altar call. Boys and girls and men and women can greatly assist in evangelism by prayer and witnessing at the altar.

There is a need for well-trained, committed soul winners or personal workers from the younger classes as well as adults. Not only is there the benefit of kids reaching kids, youth assisting youth, and adults relating to adults, but there is the ongoing training of soul winners for the future. Early instruction, preservice prayer, and consistent follow-up can result in an evangelistic Sunday school class.

The Home

Pupil's home—What a feeling of importance and self-worth a child feels when his teacher comes to visit! Lessons of love learned in the classroom take on new meaning when that pupil realizes you care enough about him to come to his home. You reinforce all you have been saying about the importance of giving one's heart to Jesus. It also provides an opportunity to get acquainted with other members of that family. Many have been won to Christ in this manner. Furthermore, your home visit better prepares you for lessons later on that can relate personally to the one visited.

Your home—Evangelism can often be carried on in the teacher's home. When you make that little girl or boy welcome in your home you can easily say that God also wants to welcome him into His home for all eternity. Friendship evangelism in your own home can be very rewarding. You can set the atmosphere for decision. A happy time of togetherness, building trust and confidence, and a good meal to satisfy body needs, can be climaxed by a time of unhurried personal conversation. The pupil will know you are interested in him as a person and will tend to listen more to what you have to say about his soul.

Camp

Perhaps more decisions are made for Christ at summer camp than anywhere else except the church itself. Very often we simply send the kids away and leave the evangelism to others. How wonderful if your class prayed for souls at summer camp. Perhaps they would like to sponsor a boy or girl as a class project. Maybe your class (depending on their age) could send some trained soul winners to the camp to serve on the counseling staff. Maybe, teacher, God is even speaking to you about this effective outreach area.

Kids at camp get as much exposure to God's Word in a week as they do in several months of Sunday school. Add to that an accepting peer group and a host of persons praying for their spiritual welfare and the climate is right for evangelism.

Retreats

Very similar to the district-sponsored summer camp is the church-sponsored retreat. Programs may vary and the staff may include some people the kids already know, but the time together and the setting greatly enhance the possibility of soul winning. When it comes to youth or young adults, the retreat is an ideal time for evangelism. Here's a sample agenda:

SNOW CAMP SCHEDULE

FRIDAY

6:00-8:30	Traveling time
8:30-9:15	Registration completion
9:30	Fellowship and film

11:00	Pizza
	Midnight ice skating
1:30	All lights out!

SATURDAY

7:30	Get up—clean up room
8:15	Breakfast
9:10-9:55	First session
10:00-10:45	Second session
10:50-11:35	Third session
11:40-12:25	Rap session—Hot Seat— Dining room
12:30	Lunch
1:30-5:00	Free time
5:30	Supper
7:30	Torchbearers
11:00	Snack time

SUNDAY

7:30	Arise—clean up room—*pack*
8:15	Breakfast
9:30	Morning worship service with Torchbearers
11:30	Leave
1:30-2:00	Return to church

Witnessing Programs

"Ye shall be my witnesses."

A small boy who grew up in the country and had few educational opportunities nevertheless became very proficient with the sling shot. He could kill a fly on the barn door, hit a frog on the edge of a puddle, or knock a bird off the limb of a tree.

He was walking one day with a man who was much impressed with his skill. The boy was pleased with the attention and responded by hitting many difficult targets. Soon they happened to pass a large nest of bees hanging from the limb of a tree. The boy just walked by.

"Don't you think you can hit the bees' nest?" asked the man. The boy replied: "Mister, frogs is frogs, birds is birds, and flies is flies, but I don't mess with them bees, they's organized."

Probably one of the major hindrances to evangelism in our Sunday school system is learning about it but never putting it into practice. The Royal Ranger who is perpetually taught camping skills but never taken on a camping trip will soon forget many of the skills he has learned and also lose interest in learning anymore. The Missionette who earns her badges on the Stairway to the Stars but never receives them will soon become disillusioned. They must also be given opportunity to put into practice the things they have learned.

In similar fashion, the Sunday school pupil who has carefully marked his New Testament, practiced witnessing in a classroom roleplaying situation, and heard constant reminders of the importance of soul winning, but has never been enrolled in a witnessing campaign, will soon write it off as an empty exercise of the church. There is a need for implementation of soul-winning skills and for organized efforts in evangelism.

AIM

Ambassadors in Mission has been a valuable witnessing program of the Assemblies of God. Sponsored by the Youth Department, this outreach for evangelism has sent witnesses into many foreign lands and key areas of the United States. Those Sunday school classes that send one or more of their members on such a program benefit by knowing they helped train the witness by sharing in prayer or financial support of that witness and by stimulating witnessing in their own group. They have a personal report on the adventure of evangelism when that class member returns.

If the AIM program is utilized in a local area or

church the entire class of prepared and qualified members can participate. The national program will gladly provide organizational assistance. In some instances E.L.A. (Evangelism Literature for America) will also provide the literature needed for an evangelistic thrust in your community. For help from AIM or E.L.A. contact the Assemblies of God, 1445 Boonville, Springfield, Missouri 65802.

Action Crusades

The Men's Department of the Assemblies of God sponsors a witnessing program called Action Crusade. By contacting your district men's director, assistance can be obtained in arranging for a crusade in your area. In some instances, this may involve several area churches. Other circumstances may indicate that your local church should sponsor such a crusade by itself.

Trained Action Crusade directors will come to your church or area and train people in witnessing or give a refresher course to those already trained. One of their witnessing tools, the Graphic Witnessing Guide, was discussed earlier in this chapter.

This is a wonderful opportunity to involve your Sunday school personnel in door-to-door witnessing. Several hours a day are spent in personal evangelism. The evenings are devoted to special services at the church. At the altars you will find opportunity to follow up on some you may have had initial contact with during the day. Some may attend who were reached by the publicity. The thrust of these services will be evangelistic in nature. This is a great time to help plant the seeds of evangelism in those from your class who have been previously unimpressed or not yet enlisted.

Community Canvass

Within walking distance of some churches and easy

driving distance for others, reside many prospects for the kingdom of God. Many times we take for granted that they have all heard the story of Christ and have already made their decision to accept or reject Him as Lord. But how do you know for sure? How can you know those who are well-churched or are just looking? Are you sure they are spiritually satisfied or could it be that they are lost?

A community canvass or census is a good way to build a workable prospect list. Suitable cards for this endeavor can be obtained from the Gospel Publishing House (1445 Boonville, Springfield, Missouri 65802) or a local Christian bookstore.

Enlist your personnel, prepare adequate maps outlining areas to be covered, and set a date, time, and place to start your canvass. Make sure that each one participating is briefed on terminology to use as he or she approaches a home. If none is suggested in the material you purchase you may want to use something like this:

"Good afternoon, my name is Cindy. I'm helping our Sunday school complete a canvass of the neighborhood in an effort to accomplish two things. First, we're trying to compile a complete list of our neighborhood family size and church preference. Second, we're making an effort not to overlook anyone who might need any services we can help with. Do you have about 5 minutes you could spare to help me fill out this informational card? Thank you so much."

COMMUNITY CANVASS

Name _____

  Last   First   Middle Init.

Address _____

Phone _____

Names of children _____

Ages _____

_____

Member of what church? _____

Attend what church? _____

Would you like to be placed on our mailing list?

Yes _____ No _____

"Well, that completes our survey. Are there any questions I might answer for you? Thank you for your time. Would you accept this little booklet as a token of my appreciation for your help? (Something nicely done and not too strong—maybe a poem.) Good-bye now. It's been a pleasure talking with you."

Don't overstay your visit unless requested to linger. There may be an opportunity to follow up at a later date. When all the cards are collected, do NOT simply file them away. Have a committee carefully go over them for good prospects and initiate a follow-up within a 1- or 2-week period. These prospects, in some instances, can be placed on your church mailing list to receive your weekly bulletin or be invited to special church services or programs.

Prospect File

As we have mentioned, the community canvass is a great start for a prospect file. You may also ask each class in your Sunday school or the entire church to submit names, addresses, and phone numbers of those they feel are good prospects. Other sources for your prospect file may be newspapers, real estate transfer notices, birth and death reports, your local utilities companies, etc. Remember, a prospect file is only good if it is put to use.

Correspondence Evangelism

Perhaps N.C.I. (National Correspondence Institute) materials are better listed under tools for evangelism, but they can also be an effective program of outreach. Overseas missionaries are tabulating thousands of conversions through the International Correspondence Institute. N.C.I. is the stateside counterpart and is available from Gospel Publishing House. There are six lessons dealing with the "Great Questions of Life." These are tremendous for presenting the gospel as the answer to life's problems.

The first lesson can be sent as a mailer to your prospect, distributed in person, or used as a follow-up for new converts. As each lesson is completed and received by your staff, the next lesson is sent to those showing interest in this program. There is a place on each lesson to submit names of others who might be interested in such a course.

Six more lessons deal with the Holy Spirit, "Your Helpful Friend." Ten lessons are also available on soul winning. These provide excellent material for training your class for evangelism.

Telephone

I was quite impressed several years ago when the Southern New England Men's Department produced a booklet called "Dial-a-Soul." Step by step it gave the words to use over the phone in winning a soul to Christ. More recently, we have participated in the nationwide program "Here's Life America," which relies heavily on the use of the telephone. In 3 weeks, using three telephones, our personal workers led over 100 persons to a commitment to Jesus Christ! These new converts were all followed up by a personal visit to their home. Several desired home visits who did not pray over the phone, and many more were saved in their own homes.

Now, such a nationwide program may not always be available together with T.V. specials, billboards, and newspaper ads, but your phone is. Any church can launch a program of telephone evangelism. Simply decide on the plan you are going to use and prepare your workers before starting. If several work at a central location they can encourage each other, but don't limit yourself to this. Your phone can be an evangelism tool all year long.

Some people have used the telethon approach with a T.V. or radio program continually reminding listeners to call the special number. I personally feel that this has been used so much as a fund-raising gimmick that we have greatly hampered its use as a tool of evangelism. Some regular programs, however, are still able to use it effectively in a talk-back situation.

Another variation of phone evangelism is a hot-line number for persons in distress. This needs to be well advertised in all the media.

Still others record Dial-a-Prayer, which meets a real ministry need. Some have tied their phone number to motel advertising, which for a price will list a special number on each phone directory in the cooperating motel. Motel customers can then dial the number and listen to the recorded message.

Every Member Evangelism

Evangelism Explosion, a book by D. James Kennedy, goes into quite lengthy detail about personal evangelism. In some situations this program may have some value. There are no doubt many other plans that will work in your situation. The important aspect as I see it is to have a plan, work your plan, and let your plan work for you.

Summary

As Jesus blessed the little boy's lunch and multiplied the loaves and fishes until everyone was filled, so He can meet our needs today. If we take the tools we have, employ them in every place we go, and keep an ongoing program of evangelism alive in our church, we too will learn of Christ's sufficiency.

There were 12 baskets of fragments left over after everyone was fed. We will also be amazed to discover that we not only have enough to do the job, we have an abundance. Christ has appointed us a task; He will also anoint us for service (Luke 4:18).

4 Pass It On

In Romans 12:6-8, the writer, under the inspiration of the Holy Spirit, reminds us to wait on our ministry—the exhorter on his exhorting; the teacher on his teaching. One of the gifts God gave the Church was teachers (1 Corinthians 12:28). The process of discipling people into the Kingdom is based on teaching as well as preaching.

The high calling of a teacher is evangelism. Paul explained it to Timothy in this way: "The things that thou hast heard of me among many witnesses, the same commit thou to faithful men, who shall be able to teach others also" (2 Timothy 2:2). In other words, "Pass it on!" No one person can do the job alone. There must be a recruiting and training aspect to his ministry.

Although a teacher may be accountable to a department superintendent, a general superintendent, an executive committee, the pastor, and the official board, his primary responsibility is to God. He is called by God, equipped by God, assisted by God, and accountable to God. This entails the compassion he has for his pupils, the dedication he employs in lesson and personal preparation, and his attitude toward cooperating with departmental and school goals and with God's stated purpose of evangelism.

A teacher's ministry is not complete after he delivers the lesson material. He has not taught till learning has taken place. He has not sufficiently taught till he reproduces the spirit of evangelism in his class. If that sounds like an ongoing task, it is. We have a continual task and we can never coast.

Training vs. Education

The three essential elements of education are: a desire to learn, something to teach, and someone to teach it. In other words, education involves a teacher, a student, and a subject to be taught.

As we look at the conversion experience of the Ethiopian eunuch, we are impressed by his desire to learn (Acts 8:26-40). Even while traveling, he was reading. He had some good subject matter—the prophecy of Isaiah. Notice Philip's question as he approached him: "Understandest thou what thou readest?" (v. 30).

Reading without understanding can prove to be an empty exercise, if not downright frustrating. A teacher is needed. With a little help from Philip, the real truth of Isaiah's prophecy was grasped, acted upon, and a new convert was soon baptized in water. Philip had something to pass on to another. As the eunuch was able to internalize its truth, there was response and reproduction. I can just imagine this new witness carrying the good news to his own country and his own sphere of influence!

Perhaps the other side of this educational coin could be termed *training*. For the 12 disciples Jesus called, His early challenge to become fishers of men was followed by 3 years of in-service training. They were with Him—they saw His actions, observed His attitude, and saw His sorrow and His triumphs.

Paul followed up his conversion experience and early testimony with a 3-year experience in the wilderness. His early travels included others who complemented his ministry. Paul followed up these tours with ministry-training trips that included young men who were still learning. He shared with Timothy, Titus, and even John Mark. Some he helped and some he lost (Demas), but he was always training (and encouraging) someone to carry on the work he found so important.

Ways and Means

This is where a Sunday school teacher has such a golden opportunity. Not only does he instruct in the history of the Bible or in the spiritual application of its teachings, but he lives it in front of his students. His enthusiasm in class, his active participation in the worship services of the church, his faithful stewardship in time and tithes, and his testimony become active ingredients in developing young lives or converts.

A teacher should attend at least two church services besides Sunday school each week. He is training by example. Those priorities he establishes for his own life will be either consciously or unconsciously transmitted to his pupils. A dedicated teacher will look for opportunities to train his students outside the classroom as well as during the Sunday school hour.

Let's look at some possible areas of training available to the Sunday school teacher.

1. *Sharing time*—A teacher who wants to train for evangelism will be in his classroom early. He will greet students as they arrive and engage in casual and personal conversation. There will be opportunities for the teacher to share individually, or with the class as a whole, his own experiences of soul winning. I might add parenthetically that if you as a teacher are not a soul winner you will never be able to effectively train your students for evangelism.

It is good from time to time to ask the students to share their soul-winning experiences. Maybe you will grow a bit weary asking for something that seems to be nonexistent, but you will be creating a vivid picture of the importance of evangelism. When someone has a soul-winning victory to share it will be a positive reinforcement for that new soul winner and a great stimulus for others in the class. A good way to get started in this is to have your class tell of those they have contacted for Christ, as well as the ones they have won.

2. *Posters*—Some teachers stimulate evangelism by attractive posters. There's a dual value here. First, we see the message the poster carries. Maybe it is informational; telling of an upcoming meeting or a special outreach ministry of your class. Perhaps it is inspirational; depicting in a scene, cartoon, or Scripture passage some soul-winning event (for example: Philip and the Ethiopian eunuch, Peter at the house of Cornelius, Andrew bringing his brother to Jesus, or one of your own class on visitation).

The other aspect of "evangelism posters" is the value received by the ones involved in making them. There is the satisfaction of service, the truth received while researching their project, and the interclass stimulation of a poster contest.

3. *Essays*—A variation of this is an essay contest on the subject of evangelism. The sharing of these essays can provide a springboard for class discussion and maybe even a classroom altar call.

4. *Roleplaying*—Drama has for centuries been a very effective medium of communication. In too many instances we have surrendered its use totally to the secular world. Or, perhaps we keep the tradition barely alive by our Christmas or Easter pageant.

Jesus was known to take a child and set him in the midst of them to illustrate a point. He used objects and object lessons. He painted word pictures—calling Herod a fox or contrasting Solomon's clothing to the lilies of the field.

No matter what age-level you teach, there are or can be opportunities to train for evangelism by roleplaying. Depict in class the evangelism of the Bible era contrasted with that of historically known soul winners of the more recent past, and then make it current by showing 20th-century evangelism. This could be a special project or a class-time starter spread over several weeks. The variations and opportunities are as broad as your imagination.

5. *Classroom practice*—After teaching evangelism methods, marking their New Testaments, and memorizing key verses, why not have your pupils break up into twos and practice leading a soul to Christ. This can be beneficial as an opportunity to personally confront every member of your class with the gospel challenge and also give each participant the feeling of experience when he meets a need to evangelize outside the class.

6. *Church altar services*—A dedicated Sunday school teacher will be an active participant in the altar services of the church. If he does not feel capable of leading a soul to Christ personally, he is unqualified to be an instructor of others. By setting an example of participation at the altar, he is training his class on a realistic level.

He may seek out a boy or girl from his own class who has responded to the appeal of the minister or he may take one of his pupils with him to the altar to either observe or participate in the winning of a soul in that pupil's age-group. The feeling of helping to win that soul is positive reinforcement for future evangelism.

7. *On the street*—From time to time there are church-wide, community-wide, or nationwide outreach campaigns. An alert teacher won't wait to be personally solicited by the pastor or campaign chairman but will seize this as an opportunity to teach evangelism to his class. Whether it be distribution of

pamphlets, placing of posters in key locations, or actual door-to-door witnessing, students can be involved. A class can take responsibility for a certain area of the city or a special part of the outreach campaign. Class members can learn by doing and share by caring. What a glorious opportunity is before us!

8. *Letter-writing evangelism*—Pupils can be encouraged to share the gospel through the mail. Perhaps each one will want to write to a special friend. Some classes may wish to concentrate on one individual at a time. Whether the writer feels a desire to explain salvation in his own words or merely includes a tract or article in a friendly letter, is not crucial. Doing something is.

9. *Seasonal opportunities*—Evangelism opportunities will vary with seasonal events. Each opportunity for the experienced soul winner is a training experience for the beginner.

New Year's Day and the early days of the new year speak of new beginnings. Birthdays of our nation's greats are opportunities to evaluate true greatness. Valentine's Day and its interest in love for one another leads easily into Calvary love. Easter is an excellent time for mini-pageants, scenarios, and posters to set the atmosphere, as well as share the blessed story of the living Christ. Pentecost Sunday is the birthday of the Church. On one such day my young people and I canvassed the entire neighborhood with appropriate literature and invited the people to share in our birthday celebration.

Children's Day activities can bring many parents to church to view a special program and thus hear the gospel. Your children receive training on how to share Christ at the same time.

The Fourth of July speaks of liberty, and is a great time to tell of Christ's liberating power. Children are trained to appreciate their heritage, dedicate themselves to keeping their land free, and learn afresh the principles that made America great. A dressed-up "George Washington" can quote the prayers of our first president and give instruction to his troops. The child is thus trained to associate right principles with good government and not to think of evangelism as strictly a "church" situation.

Vacation time is an opportunity to teach vacation evangelism. State parks, resort areas, church camps, and V.B.S. are all great training places and events.

On Labor Day we stress the needs of the working man. Politicians stand in line at factories asking for votes. What a great place to take a class of eager evangelists with attractive pieces of literature prepared with the laboring man and woman in mind.

Thanksgiving is filled with numerous outreach opportunities. Reenactment of early Thanksgivings can point out the dependence of the colonists on Christ. Baskets could be prepared for families in need and Scripture portions inserted. A teacher who takes his pupils with him on individualized missions of mercy is training them in practical and spiritual evangelism.

Christmas gives similar opportunities for basket evangelism. It is also probably the best time of year for total Sunday school involvement in a portrayal of the Christ child. As parents gather to hear Christmas recitations, sing carols, and watch the pageants, pupils are trained to openly share Christ. If possible, arrange a time for parents to visit their children's classrooms. Share with them appropriate literature. A bridge for future evangelism can be built in this way.

What else should we employ in training our pupils for evangelism? Everything possible: an open house, special projects, Parents' Day, Western Day, Baby Sunday, "This Is Your Life," contests, a time machine, space flights, sports marathons, olympics, etc. Philip started where the Ethiopian eunuch was reading and from that very place preached Jesus Christ. We must find out where our prospects are and from that point of familiar reference preach Christ.

Motivation

Some teachers find extrinsic motivation helpful in stimulating their pupils to action. They plan exciting contests with desirable rewards. Carefully they explain the rules and analyze problem areas. They point out that God himself operates on a basis of rewards.

Other teachers prefer intrinsic motivation. A job well done is reward enough. They make the evangelism efforts exciting in concept and carry-through. They endeavor to create compassion for souls in their pupils and also to show our stewardship responsibilities.

While each teacher is an individual and must find a method of evangelism that he feels comfortable with, he must also remember that each of his pupils is an individual and may have personal preferences too. It seems wise, then, to employ a multifaceted approach. A variety of activities, methods, and personnel should be used. Extrinsic and intrinsic motivation should be employed, with an overall dependence on the Holy Spirit for personal guidance.

5 Lively Stones

"Ye also, as lively stones, are built up a spiritual house, a holy priesthood, to offer up spiritual sacrifices, acceptable to God by Jesus Christ" (1 Peter 2:5).

For many years Assemblies of God Sunday schools and Word of Life literature have been endeavoring to build a wall of faith. Sound doctrine, well-researched and carefully structured lesson materials, and applicable illustrations have been the basis of curriculum.

In the minds of some, the teacher who is well versed in lesson content and is capable of stating the required amount of Scripture and commentary in a designated time period is successful. Others, however, stress that we have not taught until learning takes place, and that requires a teacher and curriculum to be pupil-oriented.

For a Sunday school to reach the broad spectrum of today's society—young and old, rich and poor, married and single, native and foreign, male and female— requires total mobilization. I guess we have to begin with the structure.

A statement of purpose is needed. A philosophy of outreach should be clearly defined. There must be sufficient classes to meet myriad needs, and regular planning and evaluation sessions to keep us on target.

The Bible illustrates this in Ephesians 2:19-22:

Now therefore ye are no more strangers and foreigners, but fellow citizens with the saints, and of the household of God; and are built upon the foundation of the apostles and prophets, Jesus Christ himself being the chief corner stone; in whom all the building fitly framed together groweth unto a holy temple in the Lord: in whom ye also are builded together for a habitation of God through the Spirit.

There must be a foundation; that's Christ. A building or structure has to be put together; that's the body of Christ (and also our Sunday school organization). As 1 Peter 2:5 states, we are "lively stones." This signifies that we possess the endurance of solid rock, while yet being alive and mobile. The solidarity of a wall is evident, yet the living characteristics of humanity demand flexibility in application.

Statement of Purpose

The national Sunday School Department has outlined their statement of purpose in a small pamphlet that you can receive by writing to the Sunday School Department, 1445 Boonville, Springfield, Missouri 65802.

A possible statement of purpose could be:

It shall be the purpose of the Sunday school of First Assembly of God of Anytown, U.S.A., to fulfill the Great Commission of Jesus Christ as stated in Matthew 28:18-20. As the educational arm of the church, we shall endeavor to accomplish this through classes that are doctrinally sound and geared to reach all members of all families regardless of race, culture, age, or position. Though instructional in nature, our purpose is the evangelization of the lost and the discipling of the saved into the body of Christ.

Philosophy of Outreach

An example of a philosophy of outreach is:

Our philosophy of outreach shall be the involvement of the total Sunday school to minister to the total man and to all persons in our community. Believing that God has made provision for the salvation of all men and recognizing that each man is different, we shall gear ourselves to a multifaceted approach in evangelism. We will train ourselves in personal evangelism and provide opportunities for witness.

We will schedule special activities and extend an invitation to all. We shall endeavor to build a support base for evangelism in our curriculum, teacher training, and Christian stewardship responsibilities. We shall give family life high priority in the planning of curriculum and the scheduling of events. We shall also give special attention to the fragmented family, i.e., the single adult, the parent without a partner, the senior citizen, and the economically and politically displaced. We will have sufficient classes to meet a variety of needs.

Grouping of persons simply by age or grade in school may be feasible for some, but is totally inadequate in other situations. Perhaps you need to consider some of the following:

1. *Nursery*—Provides a curriculum for those 6 months old and up. This is not just a baby-sitting job.

2. *Classes for newcomers and new converts*—Children who have never had the basis of the early years in Sunday school need a quick overview of the Bible before being placed arbitrarily with those who have had years of Biblical exposure. New converts need an overview of basic doctrines before they are ready to be integrated into the regular lesson cycle.

3. *College and career*—Those who are being exposed to issues of conscience and faith need a class of peers who can help them. The class needs to be flexible enough to deal with a problem faced that week on campus or at work. This does not mean a total rap session with no structure, but a keen awareness of personal needs.

4. *Ladies or men only*—Some people open up more in this type of setting. They may ask questions they would never ask in the presence of their spouse.

5. *A variety of adult classes*—These may reflect

personality differences or age differences. Electives permit a choice of subject matter.

6. *Bible quiz class*—This relates to youth and teaches a lot of Scripture.

7. *Teacher-training class*—Some have grown to the point that they now desire to serve. They need special training to equip them for this.

8. *Advanced Bible study*—This could follow the Berean correspondence courses provided through the Department of Education of the Assemblies of God.

9. *Special family classes*—Youth and parents meet in different classes but study the same subject matter (on different levels) which relates to common problems.

10. *Leadership-training classes*—Just as we need teachers for Sunday school, so we also need Royal Rangers leaders, Missionettes leaders, and various other departmental leaders.

11. *Single adults and/or single parents*—This group is often lonely and needs special attention. Most general curriculum deals with problems they do not face and ignores the ones that are very real to them.

Regular Planning and Evaluation Sessions

"Think time" is important. It is very important that the Sunday school executive committee, and at other times the entire staff, meet to evaluate their goals and accomplishments. They need to evaluate their actions in light of their purpose and in accordance with their philosophy of approach.

Panic planning should be avoided. It usually becomes a patchwork of previous programs and lacks creative effort. Regular evaluation and planning sessions aid communication, stimulate ideas, share vision, and advance evangelism.

Recognize Individual Personalities and Needs

In 1 Corinthians 12:12-18, we have a graphic description of a body that consists of many members. Each member is different in type and function, yet the body is dependent on all. The evangelistic thrust of the Sunday school must be geared to recognize differences, confess a need for variety, and address itself to a complex society.

You may well say: "That's easier said than done. How can I interpret behavior and categorize it into curricular needs. Where can I find help in assessing what classes are needed in our Sunday school and which ones stereotype people into misfitting molds?"

Written Helps

One of the obvious helps available to every Sunday school worker is an abundance of written material:

1. *Local church library and pastor's study*—Many churches have through the years amassed a variety of books, pamphlets, and articles dealing with age-level differences and social characteristics. If you don't have a library or Sunday school supply room, your pastor may have some books that will meet your needs.

2. *Community library*—A wealth of material is available at a city or school library, and many times a librarian is more than willing to help you with your need. They may also have current studies on population-growth history and projected patterns, industrial trends, and political resumes.

3. *Periodicals*—The *Sunday School Counselor* is always full of helps geared to recognition of personalities and age-levels. District bulletins with a Sunday school page can be a good source. The *Pentecostal Evangel, Christian Life,* and the *Christian Reader* can aid in personality awareness.

4. *Newspaper*—The local newspaper may be one of

your best sources of contact with the community. It carries records of births, marriages, deaths, and special news. Letters to the editor give insight into how different people think.

Community Awareness

Profiles of basic areas of community need can sometimes be gained by conversation with workers in your community service agencies—child placement, welfare, rehabilitation centers, crippled children foundations, employment bureaus, jails, and social security offices.

Labor and Management

Studies of employment needs and labor trends can give indications of a need for evangelism.

I recall a strike in a town where I was pastoring some time ago. It was not generated on the local level but dictated by the national office. I discovered that some people were in real need and asked God for guidance as to how the church could help without becoming politically involved.

We took a special offering with which we bought a large supply of bread. I took this to the local union hall and requested that it be shared with their most needy families. It may not have been much in relation to the total need, but it did say we Christians care. Our community's response was most gratifying.

Tours of factories can give us insight into the conditions our Sunday school adult pupils face day in and day out. We can better direct our evangelistic thrust when we know our people and their surroundings.

Personnel Who Can Help

Pastor—Locally you can always talk to your pastor.

He may be able to share with you, without betraying a confidence, the reason you are having a problem with a particular pupil. A time of prayer together for the direction of the Holy Spirit in helping you meet the needs of the many personalities in your class may be the most rewarding half hour you have spent in some time. The Bible does tell us that if two or three agree as touching any one thing it shall be done.

Sunday school superintendent—A key individual in any Sunday school is your superintendent. He must feel the heartbeat for evangelism to successfully orchestrate a program to help accomplish it. He stands ready to share with any of his teachers in matters of personality recognition. Some churches also have a Christian education director who can help you.

District director—Each district of the Assemblies of God has a Sunday school director. In some instances it may be his only job, in many it will be one of several responsibilities he or she carries. They stand ready to assist anyone with a sincere inquiry relating to outreach in your total community.

The national Sunday School Department is staffed with a dedicated and capable group of specialists in each age-group or special-interest category. In many instances they already have printed brochures dealing with your specific questions.

Seminars—Sunday school seminars and conventions are loaded with helps and inspiration for evangelism. Class sessions deal with pupils' needs and suggest ways of meeting those needs. Leadership seminars under the auspices of the national Sunday School Department bring this help to your local area.

Teacher initiative—I have not saved this suggestion till now because it is less important, but because it is so vital that it needed to be approached after careful surveys of where you fit into the total picture. As a teacher you need to know three things: God, your lesson, and your pupil.

1. Know God—Unless you are a current and dedicated Christian you cannot be a teacher of Sunday school. Your knowledge of God must be more than history. You must know Him in spirit and in truth. This suggests a consistent prayer life, a serious study of your Bible, and a testimony above reproach.

2. Know your lesson—You need to know your lesson. General knowledge accrues. Titles of certain Bible stories may suggest to you that you already know this topic and don't need to prepare too diligently. Each writer of curriculum has a different style, however, and you need to become familiar with it. Every lesson possesses the potential of new inspiration if given time and opportunity.

Being bound to a lesson quarterly can destroy a teacher's personal contact with a whole class or even one individual. Know your lesson well enough to permit the Holy Spirit to direct you, without the frustration of feeling unprepared. Know your lesson not only historically or in a literary sense, but also with a "feel" for how application can be made to the lives of your pupils.

3. Know your pupil—That brings me to the third thing you should know. You need to prepare your lesson with faces in mind. How does each verse of Scripture or each illustration serve to meet your goal of personal evangelism for pupils in your classroom?

a. Observe—First, I suggest that a teacher be an observant individual. Watch for signs of lost interest which may indicate lack of understanding. Be alert for behavior that says a boy is starved for attention. Observe the strained looks on a girl's face which say, "The subject matter hurts because it is missing in my life."

Listen for reading disabilities that may reflect little home support or some emotional or physical defect. A pupil's dress, attitude, peer-group relationships, and lesson participation can begin to build a mental file of that individual's needs. You can then seek God's help in reaching that person for Christ.

b. Visit—Every teacher should visit the home of every pupil. It may take a little time to accomplish this but it should be a goal we strive diligently to meet. How differently we will think of little Susie after we have seen her home broken by divorce and realize she's starved for love and security. How much more understanding we will be of Johnny when we hear his parents' priorities that seem to exclude God. What compassion for the lost is stirred when we realize our class may be the only Christlike atmosphere a child enjoys during the week. Get to know your pupils in their home setting and not just in Sunday school.

Find Qualified Personnel

The search for qualified workers in Sunday school is a continuing task. It requires relentless effort on the part of administrative leaders who place a priority on evangelism.

Potential Teachers' Class

Perhaps one of the best sources is a continuous training class in your church. Following the criteria for Sunday school certification, which encompasses the 4-part Fundamentals for Sunday School Workers or books on equivalent subjects, a Sunday school can prepare an adequate staff. The teacher of this class should be a soul winner and impart his burden of evangelism in every class.

Special Campaigns

Occasionally compassionate soul winners will surface during a revival campaign, community outreach, or district-sponsored witnessing program. These persons should be enlisted in classes to make them well-rounded as teachers and put to work.

Other Departments

There are many departments in a church. Sometimes we categorize individuals in one area and overlook their potential as Sunday school teachers. I'm not suggesting that we compete for key personnel, but simply that we evaluate the natural affinity of some persons to work in more than one area. For example: a man with a burden for boys could work with Royal Rangers and still teach a boys' class as well.

Congregation

In the congregation sit many men and women who are reasonably successful at their secular jobs. They may not be aware that they already have basic skills that could be transmitted to a classroom. Drop a seed thought in their mind. Let it germinate and then make a sincere effort to enlist them. Let them know that training is available and they will not be thrust "cold" into a teaching situation. Let them do some classroom observation or perhaps become a helper for a while until they build self-confidence.

Transfers

Occasionally you may have a family transfer from another church. Check their credentials and if they qualify, put them to work.

Calendar Planning

If we are to use the whole Sunday school to reach the whole family, we will have to give attention to a master calendar. Consideration must be given to the total church program, the distance people live from the church, work schedules, vacation time, and major community and school affairs in which your staff and students may be involved.

Before your Sunday school year begins it is good to ask yourself what you hope to accomplish during the coming year. Establish clear goals in the categories of total family, single adults, college youth, students, parents without partners, shut-ins, senior citizens, and the handicapped.

Once these goals have been established, ask yourself if any event can meet the needs of more than one category. Look for natural relationships but don't force them. Check your district and sectional or zone activities to see if some of your goals could be met by cooperation with others without sacrificing local outreach. Camps, banquets, conventions, seminars, and caravans may bring welcome assistance and not conflict with your basic goals.

Tool out the needed programs to meet your stated goals and prepare a suggested calendar of events for your Sunday school. As soon as possible, check these with your pastor and inquire about your total-church calendar-planning meeting. You may have to adjust a bit to cooperate with the other departments and some of their plans. You may even discover that some of your goals coincide and you can plan mutual evangelism activities on a co-sponsored basis.

Review your calendar often to update and inform your total staff. Let your calendar be part of your promotion and dictate the timing of the remainder.

While planning your calendar, remember that families need time at home too. Try to keep at least one night a week open. Don't plan for a beginner activity on Monday, a primary activity on Tuesday, church on Wednesday, a staff meeting on Thursday, youth on Friday, and adults on Saturday all in the same week, and then cry about fragmented families. Wherever possible schedule your activities to keep travel time for the family at a minimum.

Age-groups

Families

A family is a mobile. Thus states Edith Schaeffer in her book *What Is a Family?* (Old Tappan, NJ: Fleming H. Revell, 1975). The family is ever-changing, yet always linked in some beautiful way. Every family is a constantly changing entity. Infancy is replaced by childhood. Adolescence gives way to youth and maturity. In-laws and grandchildren all become part of the extended family. Every circumstance a family meets affects each member in a different way, but also affects the whole.

Even as each family is a changing set of persons and circumstances, so is our world. Today's family faces new sets of tests in our changing society. The clear-cut roles of our pioneer father who shot the game, tilled the fields, and built his own log cabin, while his wife raised the children, cooked the meals, and played school teacher and nursemaid, are now no longer so clearly defined. The complex pressures of triple-shift industry, mobile society, educational and political travail, and slipping moral values threaten the first of God's basic institutions.

One has said: she was born in a hospital, raised in a school, ate in restaurants, worked in an office, fellowshiped in a church, and would be buried by a funeral parlor. She didn't need a home, just a garage.

I believe the church must seize the initiative in our fragmented society and reaffirm the importance of the family. It must affect our concepts, calendars, priorities, and programs. There are books on this subject and neither time nor space permit an adequate treatment of it here, but a few suggestions are in order:

Recognize families. We have lauded the worth of individuals and their rights. We have proclaimed personhood almost to the point that we would deny the Incarnation. Jesus was born of a woman. He lived as a man. Jumping back to Creation we read: "Male and female created he them." We don't pray: "Our person which art in heaven." We proclaim role function and pray to "our Father which art in heaven." We exist for one another and need one another to be complete. Let us as Sunday school teachers and workers lend dignity to the family by recognizing them as such.

Honor a family occasionally. Perhaps a "family of the month" could be featured in your bulletin and their picture placed in the foyer in prominent display. If a "family of the year" is selected, plan a segment of time either in Sunday school or at a Sunday school banquet and give them recognition. This upgrades the status of the family.

The superintendent might start the special recognition ceremony by giving a definition of the family and a few appropriate remarks. A committee could present a "This Is Your Life" sequence for the entire family. Scripture passages relating to the family could be read and a poem or reading could follow. An appropriate plaque or gift of lasting quality could then be presented. Let the news media know what you are doing and help combat the bad publicity families are now receiving in our society.

Family-centered Curriculum

Careful attention needs to be given to curriculum. Use material that not only teaches eternal truths, but also practical applications to family living. Some electives are now available from Gospel Publishing House.

Other materials may have to be supplemental in nature. In the resources section at the end of this book I have listed several that relate to the family.

Use films that deal with family life occasionally as a supplement to your curriculum. Some good tapes are also available for certain age-groups. These could be obtained through your library.

Provide Helps for Families

Every Sunday school could provide a resource pamphlet or book for the families it serves. Whether this is a mimeographed sheet or a 90-page book, it is a light in the dark for families grasping for help. The Cathedral of Tomorrow in Akron, Ohio has a beautiful book called *How to Have a Happy Home.* It deals with the things families face and gives Scripture references as well.

What should you include in such a book?

1. A list of books, tapes, and films you have on hand.

2. A bibliography of suggested helps available through a catalogue or local bookstore.

3. A listing of local service agencies designed to help families: "Family Services," crippled children foundations, counselors, Social Security offices, the unemployment bureau, nursing homes, hospitals, etc.

4. Names of persons in your church to call for certain types of needs.

5. Scriptural references for a variety of situations.

6. Sections on all ages of the family, from the cradle to the grave.

7. Assistance in making budgets and wills.

Helps should also be made available for families to use on a family night at home. Sam Henning has written a resource on this which is available from Gospel Publishing House.

Seminars

Occasionally it is good to hold a seminar that is

geared to reaching the whole family. This works fairly well on a Saturday. Sunday school staff workers can be preassigned areas of responsibility for the program. A guest speaker can be the program feature and a family dinner, the climax. Don't segregate age-levels during the seminar, have families sit together.

Other times you may want a seminar speaker who will concentrate on one age-group or area of family life. This could be geared to parents or children, men or women, etc.

Socials

Often we gear our parties or socials to a particular age- or interest-group. This has value from a peer-group standpoint but only up to a point. If we are ever to learn from one another there has to be a "mix." Socials can be a free-and-easy time for this "mix" to occur. Plan family-type games. Eat as families. Tell the most humorous incident that has ever happened to your family. Share a blessing that has happened to your family. Show a family-type film. Have a family show a few slides of a vacation together, etc.

Communion

One of the most rewarding Christmas Eve services I have ever enjoyed was serving Communion to families as they knelt at the altar. It took 3 hours but was extremely gratifying.

Families are important. God planned them. They are under attack and the Sunday school and church must work together to reinforce them. Make Family Day at your Sunday school the biggest day of the year.

Single Adults

Not everybody is married! I know most of our func-

tions relate to couples. Our curriculum doesn't face up
to all the problems our singles face. We have to supplement. And that's not always bad—it leaves room for
creativity. Maybe we forget that there is more than one
type of single adult.

Never Married

They are not all looking for sympathy, they are looking for acceptance and understanding. Some have become disillusioned with marriage because of rising
divorce rates. Others have chosen to further their education or have chosen careers that would put undue
stress on marriage.

Jesus said in Matthew 19:12:

> For there are different reasons why men cannot marry: some,
> because they were born that way; others, because men made
> them that way; and others do not marry because of the Kingdom
> of heaven. Let him who can do it accept this teaching *(TEV)*.

What we need to recognize is that many single adults
have valid contributions to make to the kingdom of
God. We should plan classes and functions that are
designed to help them be what God wants them to be.
Make them comfortable and don't let them feel like a
fifth wheel.

Formerly Married

This is a rapidly growing number in our midst. The
fallout of our society is affecting us. Many are turning
to the church and God in this crisis hour of their lives.
We must make efforts to be nonjudgmental. Our task is
to help these people with broken hearts and shattered
dreams find new goals in life. We must help them
rebuild their concepts of self-worth and eternal value.
To do this we must:

Be accepting—Jesus called each of us as we are and

makes us what we should be. Love wins. Our manifestation of the love of Christ can help to ease the pain of rejection that they feel. We become their family. It is important for us to know they will have months of difficult adjustment after separation. They are learning how to cope with loneliness, fear, self-doubt, and changed finances and surroundings.

Be available—With an entire Sunday school to draw from, you would think there would be an abundance of ready-made funds. But this is not so. We each have our own little world and prefer not to get involved with someone else's problems. As leaders we must encourage our pupils to make themselves available for conversation, prayer, and guidance. We must be available to help them adjust to a new life.

Be Christian—Not holier than thou. Sometimes we gossip. Sometimes we warn others to stay away from certain people. Why? Either we are terribly insecure ourselves or we do not care about others. Jesus came to bind up the brokenhearted. We have been given a ministry of reconciliation. Christ has the answer for every man and woman.

Be helpful—Children of the formerly married need to be involved in our activities. Teachers should alert the parent who attends Sunday school that there are departments of the church where his or her children can find meaningful activity—nursery school, day school, Royal Rangers, Missionettes, Sunday school class projects or socials, etc.

We must be careful to provide opportunities for companionship in a nonthreatening environment. Encourage group situations as an alternative to dating in order to find friendship. Provide helps regarding finances, decisionmaking, vocational guidance, the process of grief, and spiritual assistance in the midst of suffering.

Widowed

The third group of single adults is the bereaved. A lifetime of companionship is suddenly gone. Grief turns to loneliness and loneliness to despair. Someone needs to be a friend to those in distress. The Sunday school can appoint a caring committee. These persons should have some training in what a widow or widower faces—probate court, change of living status, Social Security red tape, sale of car or home, moving to someplace less expensive, and many other problems are faced in a time of high emotional stress.

We can be the listening ear, the helping hand, and the wheels of transportation. We can provide prayer, encouragement, fellowship, a hot meal, the resources of the community, and our personal friendship.

Classes in Sunday school must be made meaningful to all three groups of single adults: never-married, formerly married, and widowed. If we discover that our particular class structure is dealing with every problem but the ones they are facing, we must have the courage and initiative to develop new classes and provide useful curriculum.

Senior Citizens

One of the most important minority groups in our midst is the senior citizens. They face loneliness, adjustments, and fear. Doctors call the fear of aging "gerontophobia." It can be a crippling disease. No matter what you call it, most persons dread growing old. The unknown appears on the horizon as an enemy that cannot be conquered.

We in the Sunday school need to address this problem with vision and determination. Senior citizens need friendship and patient understanding. Classes should relate to their needs:

1. How to survive alone.
2. God's methods of relating to others in strange settings: low-cost apartments, nursing homes, or the home of a son or daughter.
3. Facing death without fear.
4. Finding areas of usefulness during old age.
5. Coping with a changing church and new faces.
6. How to prepare a will in light of Christian stewardship.

Senior citizens can probably be grouped in 3 categories:

The Churched

For these senior citizens in our churches we need to give attention to the programs we plan, to make sure that they are included and recognized.

Classes—Use large-print quarterlies. Plan supplemental materials that relate to practical needs. Have special guests occasionally who relate how they met certain problems of old age.

Socials—Senior citizens don't want to be left out. They need to be included in our special activities. Programs occasionally need to recognize the older citizen and be geared to his needs.

Special days—Holidays are sometimes lonely days for those senior citizens whose families are now fragmented. Having children's classes prepare treats or programs for them can help fill this void. Once a year we set a Sunday aside to honor the senior citizens. Sunday school programs and church services are geared that day to minister to them. Following the morning worship service a dinner is served in their honor.

Some churches have planned a monthly program for senior citizens, complete with brief tours, recreation, shopping, and dinner. By ministering to these needs it is possible to reach other members of the extended family.

Shut-ins

Those who have been connected with our churches but are no longer able to attend our worship services need a different type of attention.

Extension classes—Th need for regular times of Bible study and Christian fellowship does not diminish with age or health. Having an extension department with a departmental superintendent and several teachers goes a long way toward filling the gap. The national Sunday School Department has a filmstrip presentation that relates well to this ministry.

Regularity is important for older citizens. They forget things so quickly, that you may become frustrated just reintroducing yourself. Also, you will probably have to listen patiently for a while to a bit of scolding for not having come more often.

The extension class on a weekly basis helps fill this need for something and someone to relate to. It is also important to the whole Sunday school to realize that they are fulfilling the call of God and not neglecting a portion of their responsibility.

Pastoral care—Perhaps a bit removed from the structure of Sunday school, but important nevertheless, is pastoral care. This ought to include Communion as well as the regular visits of the pastoral staff. The Sunday school staff in planning its programs should check with the pastor to schedule their ministries to supplement what is already being done. Days of visitation should come on the days in between pastoral visits.

Departmental ministries—All departments of the church should be concerned with the shut-ins. It is important for us to have good communication to avoid duplication of services or times of service.

Sunday school programs—While planning special programs for your classes to present in church, don't forget some segments that can be restaged in nursing homes or homes of shut-ins. If you can't reperform any segment of your children's program or children's choir, at least tape it. Some churches are making all services of the church available to shut-ins on cassette tapes on a lending basis. Why not tape some of your Sunday school classes and make that dear old saint feel more included in your Sunday school?

The Unchurched

Perhaps the greatest challenge we face is ministering to the unchurched senior citizen. This is the field of evangelism perhaps most neglected yet the closest to the end of the harvest. How can we get involved in this area?

Neighbors of the church—More and more we are finding our senior citizens grouped in low-cost housing projects or shut in together in nursing homes. Begin to extend your visits to the closest neighbors of the one who is connected with your church. They can be invited to join your extension classes and special programs. Similar outreach may win neighbors of shut-ins at their own homes.

Nursing home classes—Some Sunday schools have instituted regular Sunday school classes in nursing homes and hospitals on Sunday mornings. This becomes a real opportunity to minister to the unchurched senior citizen and often to their families as well.

Provide Training Time

As we have been discussing the mobilization of the Sunday school to meet the needs of the total family and special groups, you are probably asking how and when you will train the personnel to do all these things.

I believe that in addition to our annual worker's training conference we need a constant potential teachers' class. In some churches it will be necessary to have a potential Sunday school workers department. Several classes will have to be taught to prepare for ministry in specialized areas. In many instances this will have to be during the regular Sunday school hour. If you have qualified teachers in each of these areas, several classes can be conducted at once. If you have only one or two qualified trainers, you will have to train first in one specialized area and then in another.

Other churches may prefer to run these continual teacher-training classes on family night. The important thing is to provide a time and place for training. It will not automatically happen just by recognizing the need.

Summary

We were all created in the image and likeness of God. His Word tells us, however, that though we are all the same Body we have many members. Each is distinct in personality, gifts, and skills. To effectively minister to all within our Sunday school, we must recognize individual personalities and their respective needs. We must enlist and train qualified personnel to minister to all persons on their interest and intellectual levels.

As we carefully plan our church and Sunday school calendars to keep all interest and age needs in focus, we will be encouraged to see evangelism become a natural outgrowth of lifting up Christ. We should not try to think up or create everything by ourselves, lest we become frustrated. Use resource materials to help you plan programs for all special groups.

Jesus died for all people of all time in all the world. He will help us carry on the work He started by the power of His Holy Spirit.

6 Twelve Basketfuls

The people gathered themselves together as one man into the street. Men, women, and as many children as were old enough to understand, came to learn from the Book of the Law what was expected of them. This was the beginning of a great revival in the days of Ezra and Nehemiah. From daylight until noon the people stood as Ezra read from the Law, from his position on a high wooden pulpit. (See Nehemiah 8.)

In his place of leadership, Ezra blessed the Lord and the people responded with their "amens." They lifted their hands in praise, bowed their heads, and worshiped God.

A whole list of teachers and Levites helped the people to understand what was read. Nehemiah 8:8 states: "So they read in the book in the law of God distinctly, and gave the sense, and caused them to understand the reading." Conviction followed this careful instruction in God's Word. It was evidenced by the weeping that spread through the crowd.

This beautiful picture of revival is challenging to us today. True revival must be based on God's Word and people must be helped to understand that Word. But what about those who are not present when such a service is in progress? And what about tomorrow when the emotion of the present is forgotten? Nehemiah's instruction is classic: "Go your way, eat the fat, and drink the sweet, and send portions unto them for whom nothing is prepared" (v. 10). This instruction was carried out and the joy of the Lord became their strength.

The story does not end there. On the day following, key people were gathered together as a follow-up committee (v. 13). They discovered that not all of the Law was being followed. They began to publish and proclaim this follow-up instruction and the Feast of Tabernacles was restored. Verse 18 declares that day by day, from the first day until the last, he read in the Book of the Law.

The revival continued with confession of sin, restitution, loud crying, and the exhortation to stand and praise God with prayers and with testimony. This led to a new covenant with God and the commitment of many to that covenant.

In the Book of Esther, we read the story of the marvelous deliverance of the Jews. Haman is hanged, enemies are eliminated, and Haman's 10 sons are put to death. Because of the great deliverance they obtained, the Jews made a day of feasting and rejoicing. It is interesting to note that they too sent portions to one another. (See chapters 7-9.)

Matthew 14:13-21 records the miracle of the 5,000 being fed. Here too we see people involved in dispensing the provision of God, as we have previously noted. Let's follow this up just a bit. Jesus didn't let it stop there. He commanded His disciples to gather up the fragments that remained. They returned with 12 full baskets that would be used to minister to further needs.

Follow-up Is Sharing

It seems to me that we have a picture of a follow-up in these three instances.

1. When God's Word is shared it should be enjoyed not only by those who attend the meeting but also by those who miss it. Thus in the days of revival under

Ezra and Nehemiah they sent portions. A tape library, extension classes, and coffee clubs could be our 20th-century equivalent.

2. When deliverance comes to a people, it should not be taken for granted or easily forgotten. Days should be set aside for sharing the blessings of that deliverance. Thus they sent portions in the day of deliverance under Esther. Days designated for follow-up should be initiated.

3. When divine provision feeds the hungry and they are well filled, it should not encourage slackness or disregard for those who might still be hungry. Thus the disciples gathered up the 12 basketfuls of fragments for others. Names and addresses should be gathered, a follow-up committee appointed, and materials either mailed or delivered to new converts.

Follow-up Is Continual Instruction

From these same incidents we learn that those who do hear the Word, those who are delivered, and those who have been recipients of divine provision need to be followed up. There was continual instruction in the Word, publishing of tidings through the promises, and the gathering of provision for future needs.

Paul made follow-up missionary tours and wrote many letters of encouragement and instruction. Peter not only preached at Pentecost but traveled to the house of Cornelius and later wrote epistles to those he could not personally revisit. Matthew, Mark, Luke, and John not only traveled with Jesus and gave personal witness, they left a legacy behind them that has been a constant source of instruction and encouragement. They followed up their converts with reinforcement by conversation and written material.

Jesus used a follow-up encounter with the man born blind, as recorded in John 9. In His first meeting with the man Jesus ministered to his immediate need—healing. The disciples questioned: "Who did sin, this man, or his parents . . . ?" (v. 2). Jesus answered, "Neither. . . ." Man places blame; Jesus offers help.

The first reason men need to be followed up is to protect them from questioning disciples who sometimes seem more interested in reasons why than in the results of deliverance and the strengthening of those delivered.

Second, this man faced interrogation by his neighbors. They wanted to know how it had been accomplished. He plainly stated that he didn't know how, only Who had done it—Jesus (vv. 10-12).

Third, the Pharisees (religious leaders) put him through the "third degree" and not only questioned him about the manner of his healing but demanded a theological evaluation: "What sayest thou of him, that he hath opened thine eyes?" He answered: "He is a prophet" (v. 17).

Of course, the Pharisees did not believe or receive his testimony so they checked with his parents. They affirmed that he had been born blind and that he was their son, but they disavowed any knowledge of how he was healed. After all, they had their place in the synagogue to consider so they left this new recipient of Christ's blessing on his own. "He is of age, ask him" (vv. 19-23).

Nobody seemed happy that he had been healed. The disciples, his neighbors, the Pharisees, and his parents, all left him to survive or perish on his own. But not Jesus. He met this man who had been excommunicated from his synagogue for receiving help from God and expressing faith in Him. Jesus explained to him who He was. This so strengthened his faith that he worshiped Jesus (vv. 35-38).

The people we meet each day who are in need and we can help in some manner, need affirmation. They face a whole barrage of tests soon after their initial experience with Christ. It is imperative that we reach them with words of reassurance, an atmosphere of love, and instruction in the things of God.

Who's Responsible?

Everybody's job is nobody's job. If Abraham had continued praying and not left the responsibility for the final 10 in Sodom to Lot without informing him, we might well have had a different ending to the story. I don't mean to put this great man down, but he did take a lot for granted. He stopped too soon.

The primary responsibility for evangelistic programs rests with the pastor, God's man of revelation for that particular time and place. Follow-up merits his personal attention. He will need good information or data-gathering systems, adequate records to tabulate follow-up progress, and personnel trained and motivated to carry out the plan.

Directly under the pastor in the chain of leadership is the Sunday school executive committee, chaired in many instances by the Christian education director or the Sunday school superintendent. In conference with the pastor they are responsible for choosing a follow-up plan. They must then adapt it to local needs and educate their entire staff on how and when it is to be carried out. Their responsibilities should entail:

1. *Maintenance and review* of a prospect file.

2. *A file of all decisions made for Christ* through the Sunday school—classes, outreach programs, dual-emphasis revivals, etc. They may, in harmony with the total church, work from a master file with special notations of how and where these persons were reached (for example: Sunday school, Action Crusades, regular services, Royal Rangers, Missionettes, etc.).

3. *Class records*—Absentees should be carefully

noted, along with any attendance patterns that may be developing. Surveillance of staff workers must be maintained to see that their visitations and other assignments are being carried out.

Acting under the general supervision of the executive committee will, in some instances, be the departmental superintendents or directors. In other churches, it may be the teachers and helpers directly. Their duties get closer to the persons to be reached. What are their responsibilities?

1. Know what plan their church or Sunday school has adopted.

2. Familiarize themselves with the program—data cards, decision slips, attendance records, days of visitation, areas of geographical assignments, follow-up materials, etc.

3. Carry out the plan on a consistent basis. Fill out class records, make phone calls, send cards, make visits, report results, and evaluate effectiveness.

Some classes may well organize themselves with a full contingent of committees and offices. Assignments for follow-up of absentees and new converts may in some instances be carried out by these. Let me note, however, that responsibility to see that follow-up is done travels back up the line as well as delegation travels down the line. Too many times we cop-out on responsibility by saying, "It's not my job," while another soul is lost.

Areas of Responsibility

Geographical

Some follow-up plans work well when they are assigned to key persons who live in the area where a new person has visited or become enrolled in your Sunday school. Similar assignments may be made to follow up new converts or prospects. When this system is used it may involve assignment sheets given out at the church or assignments given over the phone by a person responsible for this.

Age or Class

This area of responsibility is usually carried out by teachers, designated helpers, or class members. They are the ones who probably know the person or situation best, or they are the ones that will get to know the individual in that particular class. It means a few hours spent and a few miles traveled, but it carries personal rewards.

Special Visitation Teams

Probably this works best when tied to specific events—city-wide crusades, V.B.S., Kids Krusades, telethons. Occasionally visitation teams, such as A.I.M. or Bible school students, will concentrate on a city in cooperation with a Sunday school summer thrust. Also there may well be some in your Sunday school who will find a continual ministry in follow-up.

An Opportunity Board

A board of this type can easily be made of cork or Homasote covered with burlap. Divide it into the following categories:

OPPORTUNITY BOARD

Prospect—Absentee—Shut-in—New Convert
Hospital—Needs a Phone Call—Needs a Card

The persons responsible for follow-up or visitation may want to make many of these visitation opportunities available to the whole church. Hang this board in a conspicuous place and put your information on a file card. The person who has time and vision to help that week takes the card, makes the call or visit, and returns the card with an appropriate note on the back.

Motivation

Desire has to be present or no plan will work no matter how carefully structured. But how do you motivate?

1. *Example.* Don't tell them how, show them.

2. *Testimonies or interviews.* Have someone share how he was reached by a follow-up program.

3. *Group therapy.* We get so lonely. Jesus sent them two by two. Sometimes it is good to meet together before visitation for prayer and afterwards to share. We can strengthen our brethren. This also works well if you are using phones for outreach or follow-up.

4. *Dinner.* Several churches may meet together for a bite to eat after work and prior to their midweek service. Those who participate have time to make a couple of calls before the service begins. What a blessing this is to your midweek service, especially after some gratifying results.

5. *Recognition.* Everyone likes to be recognized. Commend those who have been faithful in follow-up. Let the people know your areas of priority. Some people have a "teacher-of-the-month" program. List them in your bulletin. Have them stand up and be recognized. Send them a letter. Maybe you will want to have a similar program for your visitation team if they are different from your teachers.

Records

It's better to aim at something and miss than to aim at nothing and hit it every time.

A man who was quite a marksman visited a country

town. On the outskirts he saw a barn with a whole series of targets drawn on it with a bullet hole in the bullseye of every one. He just had to meet this super marksman. Then he discovered he was just a boy. "How did you do it?" the man asked. "Oh it was easy," the boy replied, "I just shot first and drew the targets around the places the bullets hit!"

Our church record system helps us to target our outreach and our follow-up. Records provide statistical data for our Sunday school, church, district, and nation. Combined reports determine how many chaplains we will be permitted to have as a denomination in our armed services.

These records are also important as a profile sheet of each student in your class. They are made to be used. Carefully and prayerfully we get guidance from our records. They tell us who is in our class, where he lives, how faithful he is in attendance and stewardship, and what behavioral pattern he is establishing.

Records tell us where our Sunday school has been and where it is going. They provide a ready-made prayer list for every teacher. They suggest who needs a card, a phone call, or a visit.

Careful analysis can also reveal how good a teacher you are. It is not only a report card of your class but of you as a teacher.

Follow-up to the Home

Only so much can be done in class. Getting into the homes of our prospects, pupils, and new converts is vital.

Phone—One link to the home is the telephone. One teacher says: "The squeaky wheel always gets the grease. Sometimes my pupils skip Sunday school just so I will notice them. So I often give them a call on the phone just to chat a bit and let them know I care."

Mail—I know postage is going up, but don't overlook a second- or third-class mailing permit. Bulletins, announcements, and letters help us keep in touch. A correspondence course can be an excellent follow-up tool.

Personal visit—This has to be one of the greatest follow-up approaches. There is nothing like being there face-to-face. It helps you to evaluate the situation in an instant. It says you really care.

New prospect—Maybe your visit is to a new prospect. Identify who you are. State the purpose of your visit. If you have a mutual friend or point of contact let him know who it is. Don't overstay. Leave some literature and suggest that you will return again sometime soon. Do so. This helps them to believe in you and your interest in them. Invite them to your Sunday school.

New enrollee—Introduce yourself to the rest of the family. Let them know you are glad Jack or Susie is in your class. Share briefly with them about your Sunday school and church. Let them know about your other departments and services. Find out if there are others in the home who might be interested in your Sunday school or church. Leave some literature.

Unsaved parents—If you know the parents of your pupil are unsaved you may still share much of the above, but be careful not to be pushy. Be alert for leading questions that may suggest a hunger in their hearts for some real answers. Pray before you go and have your New Testament handy in case they are ready to know more about the plan of salvation. Leave some literature.

Conflict Situations

Sometimes your visit may be occasioned by some problem in class. Don't approach the home with your mind made up as to who is to blame or with a whole series of suggestions for the parents to follow in straightening out Johnny. Have a prayerful and compassionate attitude. State the reason for your visit plainly but kindly. Let them know you are seeking their help in finding solutions to problems that concern someone you care very much about. Hopefully you will be able to conclude with a brief prayer and be on your way. Don't overstay. The fact that you came says more than many words. Look for future opportunities to reaffirm your love for your pupil and his entire family.

Maps and Addresses

Time is valuable. Don't waste it running all over town asking questions. Secure a good map of your area. Keep current addresses of your prospects, pupils, and new converts with you in the car. A few spare moments while you're on that side of town on some errand may turn out to be a golden opportunity. It will be lost if you are unprepared. When you discover you have been given a wrong address, try to correct it. Remember to let your Sunday school secretary know also.

Sample Pattern

Someone is bound to say: "I'd like to help with follow-up, but I don't know what to say." (1) Be simple; (2) Be specific; and (3) Be sure.

Here are some opening statements to get you going:

1. "Hi, I'm _____, Johnny's teacher at First Assembly of God, Anytown, U.S.A. Is Johnny home? I wanted to stop by for just a few minutes to see if he was sick or had any problems I could help him with. We really missed him in Sunday school."

2. "Hello! I'm _____ from First Assembly of God, Anytown, U.S.A. I'm part of the follow-up committee at our church and I noticed from my file that you:

... recently moved into town.
... recently attended our Sunday school or church.
... recently accepted Jesus as your Saviour.
... recently made a fresh commitment of your life to Christ.

"I wanted to stop by and see if there were any questions I might be able to answer or if I could offer help in any way. Is this a good time for me to stop in for a few minutes or should I come back later? When would be a good time? Thank you so much."

3. "Hi, I'm _____. You may remember me from *name of class or meeting*. It was so nice meeting you. I just wanted to stop by to tell you how glad we were to have you visit our class. I do hope you'll be able to come back. Do you have a few moments? I'd like to tell you a bit about our class and its planned activities. I thought also that you might have other members of your family we could be of service to.

Summary

Jesus was careful not only to minister to a person's immediate need, but to follow up with instruction and encouragement. Following His example, we must be careful to outline our specific areas of responsibility. Our job may well entail motivational responsibility, good records, and consistent follow-up.

Whether our contact is young or old, an absentee or a new convert, a new prospect or a transfer to our community, our personal interest is vital. Meet them in church or some public function, but don't forget to follow them up with a visit to their home. Let's gather all the fragments, that none of them be lost.

7 Enrollment Plus

Have you noted that Jesus did not *wait* for things to happen? He *caused* them to happen. For instance, He did not wait in the synagogue at Nazareth for the fishermen to leave their nets and volunteer to follow Him. Rather, He went where they were and said, "Follow me."

Likewise, the woman of Samaria did not have to leave her daily routine and attend Jesus' meeting—all on her own volition—before He would reveal to her that He was the long-awaited Messiah. Instead, He advised the Twelve that He "must needs go through Samaria."

Perhaps here more than in any other area the Church has neglected to follow her Lord's example. It is true we have bombarded the public with many invitations to "come." (In chapter 2 we discussed the numerous avenues of evangelism.) But what if they don't come?

And what about those who do come? Do they find that effort is not sufficient to become a member of our Sunday school?

For instance, does your school have a policy, written or unwritten, that a person must attend 3 Sundays before his name is added to a class record book? Many do. It is not certain where this practice had its beginnings. Perhaps there is confusion between requirements for church membership and for Sunday school enrollment.

The Assemblies of God Sunday School Guidelines

recommends "that a prospective member be enrolled the first Sunday he attends and/or expresses a desire for membership, and that termination be only when the person is deceased, moves away, identifies with another church, or requests it."

Let's consider just the "and/or" clause of that recommendation. It means you can enroll in your Sunday school someone who has never attended one session but has only expressed an interest in attending sometime!

Exclusive Policies

Let's look at another, albeit an unwritten one, Sunday school enrollment policy. This one says a person may be enrolled in Sunday school only during the actual Sunday school hour? Have you ever asked why? Why can't you enroll interested people whenever they express an interest—on a Wednesday night, Sunday night, or any time?

The third policy follows naturally after the first two: A person can be enrolled only in the Sunday school classroom. Again, this is an unwritten law, but its power is binding.

Do you see how exclusive we've become? We've excluded the boy who attends the Wednesday night Royal Rangers meetings, but who never attends Sunday school. We've excluded the housewife who answered the door during our last community canvass and said she never attends Sunday school anywhere. We've excluded people with whom we associate every day, simply because so far they have not accepted our invitation to be present in our Sunday school.

These policies, written and unwritten, have kept us from enrolling *anyone* (who expresses an interest) at *any time* (not just Sunday morning), and *anywhere* (not just in the Sunday school classroom).

Prospect or Enrollee?

But why clutter up the Sunday school records with the names of a lot of inactive members? Isn't that what a prospect file is for? Besides just last fall you spent time going through your records and weeding out those people who haven't attended in 13 or more consecutive Sundays.

After all, you're not interested in enrollment numbers; you're interested in attendance—those to whom you minister in your class each week, or at least somewhat regularly.

Well, let's look at what the advantages are of enrolling a person in a specific class with a specific teacher as compared to having his name simply listed in a prospect file.

First, if his name is in a prospect file who knows that he's a prospect? Does he know it? Does a teacher know that name is there as a possible member of his class? Probably not.

But if that person has consented to being enrolled in a specific class, he knows it and so does the teacher of the class.

This does several things. First, it gives that person a sense of belonging—a very basic human need. He can say, "When I do attend First Assembly, I won't be a stranger. I know who my teacher is to be and he knows I belong in his class, right from the start."

It also gives that newly enrolled member some impetus to be an attender—faithful, cooperative, and punctual. After all, he belongs!

There is also an effect on that teacher. When a person's name is duly enrolled in her class book, she feels a responsibility for that person. If he is absent she will want to send a card or, better yet, visit him. She'll pray for him too. After all, he's a member.

In short, he's not a name in an often-forgotten file in

the Sunday school office; he's a person known to a teacher.

Enrollment and Attendance

The Sunday school in general benefits from such a program. Some students of Sunday school growth tell us it is axiomatic that a Sunday school will have only 40 to 60 percent of its enrollment in attendance on any given Sunday. The 1975 Updates showed the Assemblies of God Sunday schools had 75 percent of their enrollment in attendance each week.

On the surface this sounds better than it is. For the probabilities are great that this good percentage is due to "roll-cleaning" practices. Another contributor to this seemingly good average is that the enrollment has become stagnant. No new names have been added.

If the Guidelines were followed carefully and only those who died, moved away, identified themselves with another church, or requested their names be removed, were taken off our rolls, the APR or *active participation rate* most likely would drop to the 40 to 60 percent that the experts gauge.

Increasing Attendance

Let's look at what that means in round figures. If your Sunday school presently averages 100, then this law of enrollment attendance says that your enrollment should be 200. (Again, by enrollment we are speaking of those who are on class books as active members and those who have been relegated to some inactive file.)

Now you want your Sunday school to average 200, what must you do? You must build your enrollment to 400.

Well how do you set about to build that enrollment to the necessary 400? Remember those three little words: *anyone, anytime, anywhere?*

It works like this. The next time your church canvasses a neighborhood your knock at the door is answered by Mr. Jones, a young family man. You say something like: "Mr. Jones, we have a fine young marrieds' class for people like you and your wife. The teacher is Jim Brown and right now they are studying what the Bible says about marriage and the family. They're even talking about how to discipline your children and instill moral values. May we enroll you and your wife in this class?"

Now if he indicates that they sometimes attend another church, you politely thank him for his time and leave. However, if he says you may enroll him in the class, you fill out an enrollment card right there and see that Jim Brown immediately gets the word that there is a new couple in his young marrieds' class.

Mr. Jones was enrolled in your Sunday school at 6:30 p.m. on the patio of his home. He has never attended your church, but he knows that someone there is aware of him and that he belongs. One Sunday he's going to show up in Jim Brown's young marrieds' class.

Building enrollment builds attendance. A decreasing enrollment results in decreasing attendance. It's a law just as there are laws of gravity.

To enroll 200 new people your entire Sunday school has to enroll only four people per week—as simply and easily as Mr. Jones was enrolled—during the next year. When your enrollment reaches 400, your attendance will average 200. It's the law.

But we've been talking hypothetically about Mr. Jones on his patio. Does this work in real churches with real people? It does.

A Real-life Example

Andy Anderson, whose book *Action* supports the attendance-enrollment theory, shares what took place in his church in Fort Myers, Florida, when they discovered this principle of growth:*

"Our own Sunday school was floundering; our enrollment had decreased for three consecutive years. As attendance slipped, it became more difficult to reach people for the Lord, and budget dollars remained basically the same despite inflation.

"I pledged myself to a 1-year commitment to build the Sunday school. A study of the records revealed that we averaged 40 percent of our enrollment on any given Sunday.

"Without realizing it, I had discovered a rule relating to enrollment and attendance: as enrollment increased, attendance increased; as enrollment decreased, attendance decreased.

"Our next hurdle was to discover a way to enroll people in great numbers. During the following months, we began to enroll new Sunday school members anywhere, anytime, and under any circumstances. There were two prerequisites: (1) They were not enrolled in another Sunday school and (2) they agreed to being enrolled.

"In 10 months, we had increased our enrollment from 1000 (with an average attendance of 400, or 40 percent) to 1650 (with an average of 650 or 40 percent).

"Think of it! With no large expenditure of money and time and no screening of candidates—simply by adding people to the roll—we have maintained the same percentage of attendance. The laws of enrollment-attendance worked!

"Not only have we seen a surge of new Sunday school members attending regularly, but we discovered that 80 percent came to Sunday school at least once. This new membership also served as the basis for visitation programs. We now had names and addresses of people who might never have been contacted by any church before.

"Most rewarding of all—most thrilling of all—is the fact that of the 40 percent who will now be regular attenders, one in three will be saved. We cannot be content to let people go to hell when we have a tool in our hands and a gospel in our hearts!"

This story can be repeated over and over again, as churches discard traditional enrollment policies and reach out to the men and women in their communities with an invitation, not just to come, but to belong.

You Can Do It Too!

For 1978, the Assemblies of God Sunday School Department has declared a year of outreach, based on a program called simply "Enrollment Plus." It will emphasize the law of enrollment attendance. A campaign for initiating this program with a manual for implementing it are available from the Gospel Publishing House.

A good place for your church to begin this enrollment program is to look at the demographics of your community. Who is there and who needs to belong to your Sunday school? A second place is to look at the current prospect files. Who of these can be enrolled in a class with a specific teacher to be concerned for their spiritual welfare?

Because this program works it requires your church to be prepared for growth. Trained teachers and workers, new classes and classrooms, and a quality program of Bible study are essential. Be sure you have them before you become involved in "Enrollment Plus."

But involved you must become. Nothing but compassion and concern for your community will stir you to action, "so none may be lost."

Action, a reach-out enrollment plan for Sunday school by E. S. Anderson. © 1975 The Sunday School Board of the Southern Baptists Convention, pp. ii-iii.

8 Evangelism and the Unique Situation

Shades of ominous darkness settled over the earth. Rumbles of thunder seemed to shake the very ground under foot. The piercing snap of lightning sent people looking for what meager cover could be found on the crest of this hill overlooking the city of Jerusalem. One could sense that something different, something supernatural was happening.

Our attention is drawn to a Man on a cross who is speaking to someone. What's that He's saying? "Today shalt thou be with me in Paradise" (Luke 23:43). Isn't that a little strange? Hanging there on a cross and still talking about the eternal future of somebody else! But that was the way it was with Jesus. He never forgot His purpose in life. No situation, however unique, could cause Jesus to forget the needs of others. He saved others, but himself He did not save. Evangelism demands a degree of self-sacrifice.

Peter turned a name-calling situation into outreach evangelism on the Day of Pentecost. People were saying they were drunk. They simply stood around to observe, but Peter began to preach the Word of truth and 3,000 souls were saved (Acts 2).

Paul and Silas were sitting in a Philippian jail. Not a pleasant situation at all, but the night was turned into a salvation experience for an entire family (16:23-34).

These dedicated soul winners rose above their circumstances and used their unique setting to share

Christ. On other occasions, Paul went over a wall in a basket, fought with beasts at Ephesus, suffered shipwreck, stood before magistrates and kings, and climaxed his life in a Roman prison. Everywhere he went he left a witness for Christ. Churches sprang up in the distant reaches of the Roman Empire as a result of a man seizing every opportunity for evangelism.

Some years ago in Colombia, South America, I met two men who had been placed in jail for their Christian witness. Their witness continued inside the jail as well. While the missionary was working hard to obtain a release for these men, God himself intervened. A miniature tornado picked the roof off the jail and dumped it in an empty field. Frightened jailers hurriedly turned the keys in the barred doors and released these faithful witnesses. God is still on the throne and interested in keeping His faithful witnesses on the job.

Maybe your situation is not a tornado, a ship at sea, a jail cell, or a cross on a lonely hill, but it is unique just the same. How can we keep our attitudes under control and our minds alert to reach the lost when the pressures are about to get us down? Well, God's Spirit will help, His Word has many answers, and a little advance preparation can also help.

The Building Program

These are days of church growth. Growth brings its own special problems. It has been fairly well tabulated, and I tend to agree, that a church will stifle growth when it reaches 80 percent of its seating capacity. This follows through in the Sunday school classroom as well. If we simply cram our pupils in until there is no room to move or no room to vary our format we will tend to limit growth.

Decisions on whether or not to build must be made by the church membership. Concerned teachers should, however, carefully evaluate their needs and collect them together with the entire school. Steps toward a building program should include a feasibility study. Here is a synopsis of what we did in similar circumstances:

1. Is it scripturally feasible?
   a. Great Commission (Mark 16:15, 16)
   b. Great compassion (Matthew 15:32; Mark 6:34; 1 John 3:17)
   c. Great confidence (1 John 4:4; John 14:12; Hebrews 10:35)
   d. Great compulsion (Nehemiah 6:3; John 9:4)

2. Is it numerically feasible? Review programs, population, current seating, attendance, and projections.

3. Is it financially feasible? Review your church's financial history, current obligations, appraisal, 10-year comparison sheet of membership, attendance, and finance.

Add to your feasibility study a generous supply of faith and a continuing compassion for lost souls and you have a recipe for growth. Evangelism cannot wait until your building program is complete. Sunday school workers may inspire enthusiasm in their pupils by attendance and study goals related to buildings or temples.

A tour of new facilities in progress helps kids feel like they are a part of what's going on. Kids Krusades, V.B.S., summer camp, retreats, and special programs should not be discontinued because your church is in a building program. A lopsided emphasis that diverts everything from program to facilities will soon eliminate the need for additional facilities.

While working in crowded facilities, strive to keep evangelism alive. Pray for it, work for it, plan for it, and expect it. *Keep a good attitude.* This will impress on pupils that you have a Christ who really can help in pressure situations. They'll desire a Saviour like that to help them.

Be Cooperative

If some juggling of chairs or supplies has to take place, do it with a cheerful spirit. Not only will it be a good example for your pupils, but it will also help the other teachers and promote a desire for evangelism in the entire school.

Have a Sense of Humor

Avoid too much critical analysis of your situation. Learn to laugh about the momentary inconveniences and the situations they spawn.

Have Faith

Believing is contagious. When you learn to apply faith to your building needs, you also learn how to apply it to the needs represented in your pupils' lives. Faith cometh by hearing and hearing by the Word of God. Let Him be your resource of faith.

Involve Your Class

A class that becomes involved in the building program either financially or personally begins to see it in terms of eternity. Their desire for evangelism grows as they see their part in God's total program of reaching the lost. We are laborers together with Christ in God.

Special Meetings

Praying for Revival

What unity is developed in a class that decides to meet together for a combination social and prayer meeting for an upcoming revival effort. Some classes may be mature enough to hold a prayer vigil or a round-the-clock prayer chain in preparation for evangelism. Many can assist in praying for those who will respond at the altar or in the prayer room.

Organize Greeters

First impressions are often made at the door. Make your visitors feel welcome by having a representative from your class at the door every night of the special meetings. What an opportune time to invite people to join your Sunday school class as well.

Help in Promotion

The cause of evangelism is well served when a class gets 100 percent involved. In-class promotion of special meetings can strive for 100-percent attendance on at least one night and a high percentage on every night. Assistance can be given by class personnel handing out brochures or giving phone invitations. Some churches have used "pew pastors." A person is assigned a pew and the responsibility to have it full on each night of the revival. Talk it up, pray it down, work it out. Revival is ours if we want it.

Combined Emphasis

The combined-emphasis revival varies slightly from the above. The difference is that two services go on at one time—one for kids and one for adults. The logic of this comes from children's church. Many have been reached for Christ and kept for Him through children's church. Something geared to their age-level and leading to a decisionmaking climax is blessed by God. Why not provide a similar service for children while you are ministering to adults? We have found it to be a very effective tool of evangelism, whether run by local personnel or invited guests.

The danger you must consider is keeping children too long (age wise) in the kids' setting, thus eliminating some persons from the adult service who may need that ministry and separating families who may need the total worship experience together. This needs to be kept in balance.

Empty Rooms

Some of you may face a situation of empty rooms. Psychologically you feel inadequate to fill them and thus tend to get discouraged. Discouraged persons don't make the best soul winners. Get rid of the picture of defeatism. No, I don't mean tear down the unused area. Find new uses for the extra space. Set up special interest centers. Make one a project room. Designate a room for teaching aids and use a bit of modular scheduling, which moves the kids from one room to another for different portions of your classroom experience. As growth occurs you can readjust your program to allow for more classes and less travel.

Don't let empty rooms become firetraps or garbage dumps. This is dangerous and creates a bad image of Christian stewardship in God's house.

If you are groping for ideas, you might consider making a room over into a replica of the early Palestinian's home. Some pupils could prepare the walls, some the ancient rugs, some the furniture, and some the utensils, etc. Check with those in charge first, however, before you go ahead.

Another time you might like to prepare a room to simulate the Philippian jail and dress your kids accordingly for a roleplaying situation. Such a feature could be shared with the rest of the department or school and an empty room can be turned into a teaching tool.

Multiple-use Rooms

Probably many of you are faced with the opposite situation. Your room has to be used all week for something else and you just can't project your own atmosphere. This is especially true in churches with a pre-school nursery or day-school program. Your room may also double as the pastor's study, the prayer room, or the parsonage living room. This does place limits on what you can do by way of decorations.

Be Flexible

It's amazing how many things you can prepare that can stand on a tabletop or the floor. Others can be set up for the class session and easily removed when you leave. Adapt to the decor of the room you are given. A class that meets in the restaurant next door to the church may start with coffee, but you wouldn't suggest that the kids using the parsonage living room or church prayer room be given cupcakes and hot chocolate.

Be Understanding

If the children who use your room for day school Monday through Friday happen to mar some display prepared by the Sunday school class, don't get "hyper." Pray that the message of evangelism your display projected has made an impression on some young mind. That works vice versa also. The day school must remember that God gives us facilities for total use. Like two rails of the railroad track, they may never meet, but they are both going in the same direction and together they can carry a lot of freight. Double use of church-school facilities may take a lot of passengers to heaven!

Be Creative

It's amazing what you can do when you take time to

think. Joshua was told he would be successful if he took time to meditate on the laws of God. So can we. Consider the law of supply and demand, laws of mutual respect, laws of church and Sunday school, and the laws of seedtime and harvest. Saturate your room with prayer, purpose, and praise. You will reap a bountiful harvest.

If you are using a room on Sunday that is used by someone else during the week, why not have your class sponsor a project to get acquainted with them? Maybe it could mean a letter left in each desk or storage area.

Perhaps it could be a get-acquainted social co-sponsored by the two classes that use the same room. What an opportunity for real evangelism as parents and students meet one another while bringing the kids to the party. An open house for one would merit special invitations to the other class using the same facilities. We are not competing for space, we are complementing each other's contribution.

Royal Rangers or Missionettes may also use rooms on family night that are used for day school or Sunday school. They should remember to leave the room in the condition they found it. As they live by their respective codes, their mark will be left behind them. Failure to live by their stated codes will also be obvious. Whether or not a person is influenced to join or support these groups is often determined by the attitudes they show in the use of mutually shared facilities.

Sunday school workers must also remember that many boys and girls come to Royal Rangers and Missionettes who were previously unchurched. They may have little concept of respect for God's house. A fertile field for evangelism exists here. Mutual conferences between leaders and teachers can be productive in understanding needs and desires of each group sharing multiple-use rooms.

Avoid hostile remarks when difficulties do appear, as

they surely will. Keep your evangelism priorities ever
in focus. Strive for good discipline in your group
whether you are in charge on family night or Sunday
morning. Make an effort to lead those under your guidance into a personal relationship with the Lord.

Your Role in a Town of Several Churches

Distinctive, Not Duplicative

Every church has a distinctive personality. In many
instances this will be a reflection of the combined
ministries each church has had through the years. It
will also reflect the culture and interest levels of the
various communities in a city or town.

God has given to the world a Church. It was born of
His love and purchased at great sacrifice. He has permitted that Church to be multifaceted and far-flung. I
think it is important for each Sunday school worker to
realize that we will not minister to the needs of
everyone. Neither will someone else minister to the
needs of all in our community. If God has placed us in a
place of opportunity and responsibility he has done so
for a reason. That is to help build the kingdom of God.

Cooperative, Not Competitive

There may be times when combined city-wide efforts will be useful—conventions, seminars, training
sessions, or evangelistic endeavors. There are some
things we can do together that we can never do alone.
We can be supportive in prayer and cooperative in
spirit. The Bible says we are to rejoice with those who
rejoice and weep with them that weep.

Our Role Should Be Directed

As a Spirit-led people in theory, we also need to be
divinely directed in practice. If God is the Master Con-

ductor and we each have a part to play, He will always orchestrate harmony. As we learn to lean on the guidance systems of the Holy Spirit, He will see to it that the whole city benefits by the spiritual cohabitation of His church.

The New Teacher

So you've been chosen to be a teacher in Sunday school. Congratulations! Were you told that you were a last resort? Nobody else would take the class so you just have to get in there and do your best. Maybe you're scared to death. Here are a few suggestions:

1. *Learn the Sunday school structure.* Find out who you are accountable to and what your responsibilities and privileges are. If your Sunday school does not have a written job description, at least have your superintendent give you a letter explaining some of the basics.

2. *Ask for national Sunday School Department service literature.* The national Sunday School Department has a vast supply of information on age-levels, teaching methods, and general overview of the Sunday school. They will gladly send you a supply that relates to your age-group or interest level. They can also give you a bibliography of books on related areas.

3. *Fundamentals for Sunday School Workers.* If your Sunday school has this 4-part basic course for Sunday school workers, study it well. If they don't, order it from Gospel Publishing House and study it at home. The four books cover the following subjects:

    a. Your Sunday School at Work (Organization)
    b. Knowing Your Bible
    c. Understanding Our Doctrine
    d. Mastering the Methods

This is a basic help for new teachers and provides the foundation for your certification as a Sunday school teacher.

4. *Attend all workers conferences.* Don't follow the bad example of the few teachers who think they don't need the body. Establish yourself as a cooperative team player, not an individual superstar.

5. *Read books on evangelism.* Our role is evangelism as well as instruction and discipling. Pray much and decide to be a soul winner.

6. *Study the needs of your class.* Remember that each pupil is a separate personality with a distinct set of needs. Get to know each one and plan your lessons to meet their needs.

7. *Be a Christian example.* Be faithful in church attendance and stewardship. Let your pupils desire to be what you are and you be what you want them to become.

8. *Attend seminars.* If there is a Sunday school leadership seminar or convention available to you, take advantage of it. You will learn from the displays and association with other Sunday school workers as well as the scheduled programs.

9. *Show initiative.* Don't be afraid to try something new or something old with a new dedication to make it work.

10. *Keep adequate records.* They will become your ready-made profile for class evaluation, a prayer list, and motivation for evangelism.

Summary

Not all of life is "business as usual." There are many unique situations. A majority of Biblical history was written by a few who dared to be different. This godly, faithful minority influenced a majority of history. So can you.

If you are in a building program, adjust to the situation and continue to build the kingdom of God. When special meetings are in progress, get involved yourself and involve your class. Should conditions be crowded, keep a good attitude and build enthusiasm in your class as you look forward to better conditions in the future.

Maybe you have empty rooms. Use them, then fill them. Multiple-use rooms present different problems, but none you can't cope with. Other churches are trying to reach the same town you are? Rejoice, God has others who care. You are not alone. Your role is brand-new? What a golden opportunity. God will help you become a real soul winner.

Whatever your unique situation may be, use it for the glory of God. Turn your stumbling blocks into stepping stones to victory. "Behold, [He has] set before [us] an open door, and no man can shut it" (Revelation 3:8). We will evangelize until Jesus comes in the clouds of glory or calls us home to tell us, "Well done, thou good and faithful servant" (Matthew 25:21).

Resources

Christenson, Larry. *The Christian Family*. Minneapolis, MN: Bethany Fellowship, Inc., 1970.

Dobson, James. *Dare to Discipline*. Wheaton, IL: Tyndale House Publishers, 1972.

LaHaye, Tim. *How to Be Happy Though Married*. Wheaton, IL: Tyndale House Publishers.

Osborne, Cecil G. *The Art of Understanding Your Mate*. Grand Rapids, MI: Zondervan Publishing House, 1974.

Petersen, J. Allan. *Before You Marry*. Wheaton, IL: Tyndale House Publishers.

———, ed. *The Marriage Affair*. Wheaton, IL: Tyndale House Publishers.

———. *Two Become One*. Wheaton, IL: Tyndale House Publishers, 1975.

Scanzoni, Letha. *Sex Is a Parent Affair*. Glendale, CA: Regal Publications, 1973.

Schaeffer, Edith. *What Is a Family?* Old Tappan, NJ: Fleming H. Revell, 1975.

Towns, Elmer. *Evangelize Thru Christian Education*. Wheaton, IL: Evangelical Teacher Training Association.

Wright, Norman. *Communication: Key to Your Marriage*. Glendale, CA: Regal Publications.

Helps Available From the National
Sunday School Department

"A Piece of Himself" (a filmstrip)
Calendar Planning and Overhead Transparency
Certification Requirements
Family Night Programs
Fundamentals for Sunday School Workers
101 Ideas—George Edgerly
Report on Sunday School Growth—George Edgerly
Service Literature